Engaging Difference

Engaging Difference

Teaching Humanities and Social Science in Multicultural Environments

Edited by
Dovilė Budrytė
Scott A. Boykin

ROWMAN & LITTLEFIELD
Lanham • Boulder • New York • London

Published by Rowman & Littlefield
A wholly owned subsidiary of The Rowman & Littlefield Publishing Group, Inc.
4501 Forbes Boulevard, Suite 200, Lanham, Maryland 20706
www.rowman.com

Unit A, Whitacre Mews, 26-34 Stannary Street, London SE11 4AB

British Library Cataloguing in Publication Information Available

Library of Congress Cataloging-in-Publication Data Avaliable

ISBN 9781475825077 (hardback : alk. paper) | ISBN 9781475825084 (pbk. : alk. paper) | ISBN 9781475825081 (electronic)

♾ ™ The paper used in this publication meets the minimum requirements of American National Standard for Information Sciences Permanence of Paper for Printed Library Materials, ANSI/NISO Z39.48-1992.

Printed in the United States of America

Contents

Preface

Engaging Difference, Overcoming the Fear of Otherness: How to Teach Effectively in Diverse Classrooms?

As articulated by James A. Banks more than a decade ago, "Multicultural education, as defined and conceptualized by its major architects during the last decade, is not an ethnic or gender-specific movement, but a movement designed to empower all students to become knowledgeable, caring and active citizens in a deeply troubled and ethnically polarized nation and the world" (Banks 2002, 5). This inclusive vision remains appealing in the United States and other liberal democracies, where the student bodies are becoming increasingly diverse, but political, ethnic, and socioeconomic cleavages persist.

To achieve this vision, Banks recommends several goals for educators. It is essential that students master specific skills, including reading and writing, and are empowered to become "knowledge producers," not merely uncritical knowledge consumers (Banks 2002, 4, 81). This implies that their experiences are an important part of the learning process. In addition, according to Banks, both teachers and students must develop the ability to transcend their national identities and embrace reflective global consciousness (Banks 2002, 81).

The principles of multicultural education outlined by Banks are essential for developing intercultural competence, defined as the "ability to communicate effectively and appropriately in intercultural situations, to shift frames of references appropriately and adapt behavior to cultural context" (Deardorff 2006, 249). For many teachers in the United States and elsewhere who teach in diverse classrooms, this ability has become an essential part of their job. Students come from various cultures and embrace different (and often competing) values. One of the many roles of the teacher is to communicate effectively with the students under such circumstances.

Teaching in diverse environments comes with difficult ethical, pedagogical, and philosophical questions. For example, how can teachers create communities of learning when the participants do not share the same frame of reference, such as popular culture or civic education? How should teachers pursue the traditional goals of a liberal arts education, such as holistic development, global awareness, and cosmopolitan values, in an environment where the members of the learning community may not embrace the same foundational knowledge?

There is a growing realization in different fields that "traditional" pedagogical methods (teacher-centered and content-based), which focus on the memorization of basic information and assume that students share a sense of belonging to the same culture, are ineffective in addressing divergent student backgrounds. This may be especially true in undergraduate courses in which students do not share a common social or cultural environment, language, national citizenship, or sense of belonging.

Those who are trying to develop pedagogies that support intercultural competence-building argue that reflection on teaching, peer interaction in the classroom, and other carefully designed student interactions are essential to success in diverse classrooms. Amy Lee and colleagues identify three intercultural pedagogical principles (Lee et al. 2012, 55–59). First, teachers should create and facilitate "purposeful interactions" in the classroom where diverse perspectives are valued. Second, students should be seen as resources, bringing in experience-based insights. Third, conflict is to be expected and engaged effectively and meaningfully.

The literature on multicultural education and intercultural competence puts forward admirable ideals, yet there are many challenges to their implementation. For example, many students and teachers are faced with poverty and therefore likely to experience cognitive exhaustion. (People who worry about the basics of survival are less likely to perform well in tasks that require reasoning and concentration; see Mani et al. 2013.)

Cognitive exhaustion could be linked to support for simple top-down communication. This may be an obstacle for egalitarian but complex interactions in the classroom and could explain the persistence of hierarchical top-down pedagogies.

Undoubtedly, students in diverse classrooms can offer valuable experiences and insights. But is it possible (or even desirable sometimes) to make sure that everyone feels comfortable voicing their perspectives, including unpopular views and marginalized opinions? How should teachers handle complicated situations, such as genocide denial or support for cultural norms that are not consistent with universal human rights? Do certain perspectives "deserve" to be silenced immediately? In other words, what are the limits of tolerance in the diverse classroom?

Interestingly, the increasingly diverse body of first-year college students in the United States has expressed high levels of support for diversity initiatives, including affirmative action in university admissions. The percentage who identify themselves as "right of the center" has dropped to approximately 25 percent, the lowest level since the 1990s (Eagan et al. 2016, 27). At the same time, there is a national debate about the decline of free speech on U.S. college campuses. Even President Obama in 2015 warned about the dangers of college students being "coddled" and "protected" from different points of view on campuses (Ross 2015).

Teachers who work in diverse classrooms confront challenging ethical dilemmas related to tolerance and inclusion, egalitarian communication, and sensitive topics almost every day. Their experiences can provide useful contributions to the debates in the United States and elsewhere about inclusiveness and tolerance and enrich the literature on engaging diversity in the classroom. Most importantly, these real classroom experiences can help to bridge theory and practice and offer specific suggestions about how theoretical insights from the literature on multicultural pedagogy and intercultural education can be implemented in the classroom.

This book consists of contributions by practitioners who have taught in diverse classrooms and developed teaching strategies to engage diverse student bodies. The contributors are from different disciplines (political science, business, psychology, foreign language, history, and education). Their contributions are rooted in different educational philosophies, but they share the same goal: to engage diversity effectively in the classroom and beyond. The two editors embrace different cultural values and political views but are committed to learning about the best teaching in diverse classrooms.

In terms of theory, the volume draws on several bodies of relevant literature, including intersectional pedagogy, multicultural education, and Holocaust education. Several authors (Natalya T. Riegg, Richard S. Rawls and Janita L. Rawls, Michael A. Lewkowicz, and Dovilė Budrytė) relate their work to the literature on intersectional pedagogies. These teaching strategies address such complex variables as global developments, linguistic differences, ethnicity, gender or national identity, and their combination to determine an individual's role and responsibility in a regional and global context.

In the words of Julianne Malveaux, "Intersectionality is a big word to talk about the small ways in which we live. . . . In other words, we are used to using one or two things to explain our reality, when four or five factors might influence our space" (2002, 27). Intersectionality challenges simplistic definitions of identity that focus on one category, such as ethnicity or gender. Each person is complex, and her or his identity should not be reduced to a prescribed group. However, being associated with a group cannot be separated from power relations. Historically, certain groups of people have been subjected to discrimination and abuse.

One of the main conclusions from this body of literature and the related chapters in this volume is that effective teaching in diverse classrooms attempts to recognize the individuality of every person and express respect for complexity. Scholars who embrace intersectionality as the guiding approach to their teaching are likely to practice culturally responsive pedagogy, attempting to "socially locate individuals in the context of their 'real lives'" (Berger and Guidroz 2009). Although there are works reflecting on issues related to intersectionality in the lives of students (e.g., Gallagher-Geurtsen 2009; Pérez Huber 2010), there is a shortage of works that demonstrate the application of a culturally responsive pedagogy in the college classroom. Several authors in this volume describe assignments constructed using insights from this literature.

Riegg's chapter develops an intersectional pedagogy for teaching international relations and related fields, such as international politics. She argues that the first step is to focus on the study of "ordinary individuals" in global politics. This shift is consistent with a real global phenomenon, described as the "rise of the global commoner" by Riegg. This rise implies that it is impossible to understand terrorism, the Arab Spring, and other phenomena without exploring the intersections of various identities and power relations.

Riegg asks, "What teaching methods and techniques could appropriately emphasize the cultural dimension of international politics?" Her chapter includes a detailed description of simulations that her students have been creating for years in cooperation with high school students. The students choose the topics and write scenarios about international conflicts. This activity helps them to explore the multilayered identities of people engaged in conflicts and understand what makes it difficult to resolve these conflicts.

Rawls and Rawls's chapter describes one important way that educators can recognize the individuality of students by exploring alternative ways to assess student learning. The authors observe that, in classrooms in the United States and similar cultures, many educators operate on the assumption that students have the ability to express logical arguments in writing. Assessment in many classes is based on written work. However, many students arrive from what the authors call "oral cultures," and they excel in storytelling, even if not in writing.

Rawls and Rawls argue that educators' exclusive focus on writing disempowers many students from their "oral cultures." Furthermore, the failure to write well can flow from many reasons, including dyslexia, a lack of exposure to reading and writing as a toddler, or growing up in a culture or family that prizes oral forms of communication over written forms. A pedagogical approach developed by the authors of this chapter—an approach that is inspired by the literature on intersectionality—demands that these identities be acknowledged. Their chapter includes a detailed description of how teachers can perform oral assessments.

Lewkowicz focuses on how teaching about the evolution of civil rights in the United States can be related to student lives and even help to structure class discussions about such sensitive topics as race, gender, or sexual orientation. Many Supreme Court rulings have addressed segregation, affirmative action, gender-based work hours, the right to vote, and same-sex marriage, among other issues. The language of rights in America is often the language of the law. Drawing on literature on intersectionality, Lewkowicz develops an approach to discuss these court rulings.

He argues that the literature on intersectionality has shown that individuals have complex identities that cannot be reduced to one dimension (although court decisions often focus on one dimension). To capture the complexity of identity politics, it is crucial to include a detailed historical background (context) for each court case focusing on civil rights; analyze the variables that affected the decision-making of the justices; and, most importantly, identify the direct and indirect consequences of each case for various groups in the United States (not just the one category mentioned in the case).

Indeed, deconstructing categories and revealing the multiple identities within each group have been some of the main contributions of intersectional approaches. Drawing on this insight, Budrytė's chapter describes several ways that intersectional approaches have influenced her teaching of political science classes. Instead of making generalizations about groups ("women," "nations," etc.), it is useful to think about how the complexity and individuality of the people involved in policies and political processes can be acknowledged. This approach helps to avoid negative (or positive) associations with groups of people that can have negative consequences.

Budrytė presents several assignments that demonstrate the importance of complexity and individuality in the study of political processes. The study of globalization includes not only the analysis of macrofactors (such as the impact of international trade) but also the intersection of economic (dis)empowerment and race in real people's lives. The civil rights movement in the United States can be enriched by using the oral testimonies of participants in this movement and students' own stories. The international dimension of this movement can be highlighted by using the biographies and travel stories of prominent individuals, such as W. E. B. Du Bois.

While discussing similar themes (empowerment, identities, and civil rights), several other authors (Kristina Watkins Mormino, Josephine J. Dawuni, Bryan L. Dawson, Barbara Tedrow, Ellen G. Rafshoon, and Ignas Kalpokas) relate their work to the principles of multicultural pedagogy articulated by James A. Banks. They develop culturally sensitive pedagogies, focusing on the intersection between various identities and related power relations in the classroom. Most of these authors make a case for transformational pedagogies in diverse classrooms—pedagogies that are committed to challenging hierarchies and empowering all students and teachers.

Mormino explores the issues that are associated with teaching foreign languages in a multicultural classroom. Pedagogical literature on modern language instruction suggests that language instruction is most effective when structures are studied in a cultural context. In a diverse environment (where students range in national origin, primary language, age, class, or ethnicity), it becomes challenging to employ well-known cultural references or evoke common experiences, thereby engaging student interest and avoiding translation.

In a diverse class, there may be a multiplicity of responses to a single culturally bound stimulus. A picture from the *Brady Bunch* may be useful for conveying family vocabulary, but a foreign student who has never seen the program might reasonably conclude that the image shows four generations of the same family. The resulting "cultural confusion" disrupts an accurate understanding of the vocabulary presented. The chapter suggests various ways that teachers can deal with "cultural confusion" and related challenges in class. These include fostering student respect for the cultures present in class, curiosity, and critical thinking.

Dawuni's chapter focuses on the interactions between foreign-trained instructors who have foreign accents and students in the United States. Dawuni argues that accent often becomes an "essentialized problem" in American colleges—a problem that obscures the fact that there are many other challenges and opportunities that both students and foreign-trained professors face in the classroom. Dawuni examines the intersections of culture and power dynamics in the classroom and concludes that the instructor's personal and social identities can be powerful tools in teaching.

Kalpokas's chapter also asks questions about the instructor's role in the classroom: Is an "objective," detached stance possible or desirable, especially when teaching controversial issues, such as psychological manipulation? Kalpokas describes his experiences teaching a course on the "weaponization of social media." The students in this course are required to create a plan for an "offensive social media psychological influence operation." This assignment encourages students to think critically about the instrumentalization of social media and the processes related to identity manipulation.

Dawson demonstrates one way of teaching issues related to racial identity, which can be a controversial and polarizing topic in a diverse classroom. His chapter analyzes the practical applications of Peggy McIntosh's (1993) idea of the "invisible knapsack" to discuss issues of privilege. McIntosh relates her experiences as a white woman and the unearned resources she has been given due to her ethnicity (racial identity). She emphasizes that the full collection of privileges and resources are not distributed or shared equally among people of different ethnicities, racial identities, or genders. In his classes, such as Organizational Behavior or Organizational Psychology, Dawson uses the concept of right-handedness to inspire his students to think about similar issues, including gender disparities, age differences, and ethnic perceptions among predominantly white students.

To be able to discuss similar issues effectively, it is extremely important to create a welcoming and supportive classroom environment. Tedrow's chapter describes one way to achieve this goal. She writes about a project that she led on a Fulbright fellowship in South Africa, focusing on an assignment about the favorite places of her students. The students were asked to describe and analyze their favorite places. Several related assignments were linked to the study of geography, mapmaking, writing, music, and critical analysis. Tedrow argues that similar approaches can work well to "decolonize teaching" in postcolonial settings and help students to value their own knowledge and the places they are from. The students not only rediscovered their favorite places but also found common ground with other students and teachers when stories of loss, endurance, and transformation were told. In addition, this "sense of place" teaching allowed students to appreciate cultural differences.

Rafshoon's chapter is also about how to learn about cultural differences. She discusses a strategy designed to help students to understand the complexities of immigrant experiences in the United States from a historical perspective. It uses Anzia Yezierska's 1925 novel *Bread Givers*, a Russian-Jewish *Pride and Prejudice*, with the plot centering on an Old World father's efforts to marry off his four daughters to the wealthiest men he can find. Each student is given the role of one of the characters in the book. Male students typically act as a jilted suitor or a husband; female students play the parts of the daughters, their mother, or their stepmother. The students are asked to complete an innovative writing exercise. They write a eulogy for the father from the perspective of their particular characters. The class discussion that follows is an opportunity for students to read their eulogies in a mock funeral and to reflect on how the sex and age of their characters affect their adjustment to American life and culture.

Two chapters, one by Louis Schmier, the other by Natalie Bormann and Veronica Czastkiewicz, demonstrate the continued relevance of Holocaust education to teaching about diversity. Schmier describes how he taught a general education course focusing on the enormity of the Holocaust. In this course, the "'Holocaust' was more than a noun; a label; a construct; a list of names, places, dates, numbers; a received definition to be gathered and memorized and crammed for a test." Instead, the course was designed to create relevant student experiences, not only "to individualize the Holocaust, but to personalize it."

Bormann and Czastkiewicz describe the challenges related to study-abroad trips to Auschwitz and other death camps. The authors raise two important questions. First, How can one integrate the often-traumatic experience of visiting sites of trauma into learning about the events at those very sites? Second, Is there a conflict between the ethical imperative to remember the catastrophic past and the impetus to find ways to teach about it? Bormann and Czastkiewicz argue that it is important to understand the dangers associated with students "cast into the role of trauma tourists" and suggest that educators think carefully about activities during similar trips. Their chapter makes a case for "educators as curators"—curators who choose activities for students that "may lessen both the experience as tourist and also that of [vicarious] trauma."

The remaining contribution addresses issues related to the creation of a favorable institutional environment for successful teaching in diverse classrooms. Scott A. Boykin's chapter assesses the state of the law regarding discriminatory campus speech, analyzes the balancing act colleges and universities must perform when drafting speech policies, and offers guiding principles these institutions should consider when designing policies to balance freedom of expression with freedom from discrimination. This final chapter includes suggestions for educational institutions about how to draft policies that promote free speech and thus contribute to creating a culture where diverse viewpoints are valued and openly discussed, not suppressed.

A commitment to creating and maintaining such a culture is essential for the vision articulated by James A. Banks, who argued that a major goal of multicultural education is to develop knowledgeable, caring, and active global citizens (Banks 2002). The chapters included in this volume describe various ways to contribute to the creation of such a culture. They point to several commonalities in the approaches employed by faculty teaching in diverse environments. Many authors highlight the importance of finding ways to create relevant student experiences and acknowledge their importance in absorbing and even creating knowledge. Reflection on such experiences helps to acknowledge the complexity of human beings and to avoid reproducing stereotypes about identity groups.

Although it is difficult to come up with recipes for effective teaching in diverse classrooms that work all the time, the contributions suggest that such teaching is impossible without appreciation of complexity and the acknowledgment of the individuality of each person in class, while at the same time trying to create a sense of community in the classroom (and beyond). Such teaching is neither "teacher-centered" nor "student-centered." It is based on the interdependence of students and teachers and is linked to various communities worldwide.

Acknowledgments

Dovilė Budrytė would like to thank C. Douglas Johnson from Georgia Gwinnett College and Anna Rulska-Kuthy from Brescia College, with whom she worked during the initial stages of this project. This project was supported by two faculty research (SEED) grants, "From Emotion to Critical Thinking? Teaching about the Politics of Trauma in the College Classroom" (2014–2015) and "Intersectionality as a Paradigm in Educational and Policy Settings: A Comparative Study" (2009–2010) at Georgia Gwinnett College. Research insights were presented during a seminar, "Overcoming the Fear of Otherness," sponsored by the AACU (Association of American Colleges and Universities) on April 21, 2016.

Scott Boykin thanks his wife, Susanne, for her support.

Chapter One

Intersectionality and Popular Empowerment in International Relations

Natalya T. Riegg

The literature on intersectionality challenges definitions of identity as an association with one group as overly simplistic and emphasizes instead that a person's identity may be shaped by multiple group memberships at once (e.g., Hancock 2007; McCall 2005). This chapter discusses the implications of applying intersectionality to the discipline of international relations (IR). The traditional theoretical toolkit of IR does not sufficiently capture the rising importance of ordinary individuals in the practice of international politics today and needs to be complemented by additional theoretical lenses.

SETTING THE CONTEXT

Contemporary IR theories still rarely include the issues of individuals, their subjectivities, and their life-worlds as explanatory or interpretive tools. The impersonal paradigms are understandably reflected in IR classrooms. Most IR textbooks discuss states and their systemic interactions extensively but have precious little to say about the role of individuals (Goldstein and Pevehouse 2013; Mingst and Arreguin-Toft 2013). As a result, the students often walk away with the impression that IR is a discipline for which individual human beings have very little relevance and next to no significance.

Ordinary individuals have become increasingly significant as both actors and agents of today's international politics, and this phenomenon is the rise of the global commoner. Pedagogically, the rise of the global commoner (an ordinary individual) requires a new emphasis on a "democratized" image (person) in IR classrooms, which correlates with the general tendency toward "democratization" and personalization of higher education in general and its teaching methods in particular.

DEMOCRACY AS A WAY OF LIFE

Fareed Zakaria (2007) describes a widespread, multifaceted shift of power downward, toward ordinary people, and claims that democracy has gone from being a form of government to becoming a way of life. Today the international community is witnessing even more dramatic developments along the same lines. Internationally, consequential empowerment of average individuals is no longer restricted to institutionalized democratic politics. Consider the transformative power of popular political participation, even in the absence of traditional democratic institutions, demonstrated by recent leaderless revolutions in the Arab world (the Arab Spring). Unpopular regimes were overthrown in Egypt, Tunisia, and Libya, with the Syrian leadership desperately and brutally trying to suppress popular unrest.

Thinking pedagogically, the recent history of the Arab Spring may provide a good opportunity for role-playing exercises in IR classrooms, where students may assume roles of different actors and practice the development of strategies for addressing complex issues of international concern. The rise of the global commoner manifested by the Arab Spring was matched by similar phenomena in the West, including the grassroots ascent of the populist right-wing Tea Party in 2012; the 2011 and 2012 riots in Britain and Greece; and other social movements of recent years, such as "Anonymous" and "Occupy Wall Street."

These movements or mass activities, frequently without a unifying agenda, reveal a dramatic increase in the importance of the diversity of individual agents for political processes, including foreign policy. Just as in the Middle Eastern case, the protesters are not unified in their motivations or demands but only in the personal agency of the average, common person, challenging the established social and political structures.

THE INTERNATIONAL POLITICS OF IDENTITY AND
THE RISE OF TERRORISM

The rise of the international politics of identity, including its most militant and extreme cases, such as terrorism, may be the most interesting if controversial phenomenon that, together with other developments, manifests the enhanced agency of the global commoner in today's international politics. Different types of identity politics, ranging from violent ethno-nationalism in parts of the post-Communist world to the Sunni–Shiite divide in post-Saddam Iraq (and elsewhere in the Muslim world), bloody and illiberal as they often are, represent a new type of activism by previously silenced voices. These developments demonstrate a perverted form of internalized liberal democratic discourses about individual freedom. In this sense, violent ethno-nationalism and even terrorism can be seen as "ugly cousins" of the liberal-democratic movements, carrying on, with radically different means, the similar emancipatory efforts that have been carried by the people of color, women, gays, and other historically marginalized identity groups.

To sum up, different forms of identity politics manifest self-referential, normative visions of ordinary individuals, repulsive as some of these visions and some mediums of their manifestation may be. Implicit consideration and anxiety over this sort of situation was probably at the heart of previous decades-long U.S. support for undemocratic Arab regimes.

IMPLICATIONS FOR THEORY OF THE RISE OF THE GLOBAL COMMONER IN IR

The unprecedentedly significant role of average individuals, the global commoner, in IR today implies that successful foreign policy decisions need to be increasingly informed by the knowledge of the functioning of IR on the quotidian level, as well as by the ability to establish connections between historical political events and ordinary biographies. IR theory needs to develop adequate answers to these empirical challenges and to more fully incorporate the individual. Clearly, a successful, useful analytic precedent for establishing connections between the personal and the political has been provided by decades-long feminist scholarship. Moreover, the feminist recognition of individuality, as well as the variety of political experiences, eventually stimulated the development of intersectionality.

Intersectionality recognizes that individuals are unique composites of their circumstances and their stances toward those circumstances. Individuals are normally subject to states. Individuals always have a mother tongue. In today's world, individuals always live as gendered beings, even if the simplicity of an "ethnographically innocent" two genders is replaced by numerous ones. Individuals are formed within certain educational systems. The intersections of all these and other political dimensions routinely form modern individual identities.

PEDAGOGICAL IMPLICATIONS: TEACHING INCLUSION AND INTERSECTIONALITY

Which pedagogical philosophy and methods would adequately capture the aforementioned discussion? Which teaching strategies and techniques could reflect the new international importance of ordinary individuals, with all the idiosyncratic and intriguing intersections of their identities and power? Which curriculum adjustments would be appropriate for learning more democratic and personal dimensions of IR?

There are various ways through which different peoples, as well as different people—as culturally, politically, and psychologically diverse human beings—construct their ideas about the national interests of their countries. With the enhanced importance of these people for contemporary international politics, there is now an increased requirement to take the cultural dimension of international politics into consideration as a "key expression of national identity that can affect goals, policies, and international interactions" (Fowler 2009, 342). This requirement should find its way into the college classroom.

Which teaching methods and techniques could appropriately emphasize the cultural dimension of international politics? Traditional teaching and learning methods, based on lectures and memorization of concepts, theories, and various explanatory models related to the functioning of the international system, as well as the accumulation of positive information on different regions and nations of the world, are no longer sufficient for understanding contemporary IR because they rely heavily on impersonal objectification of the subject of international studies.

These methods increasingly need to be complemented by strategies and techniques that will help students to understand the thinking and conditions of other people from faraway lands and to understand them not only cerebrally but also viscerally. In other words, in today's globalized world, with the heightened role of ordinary people in international politics, the IR instructors are challenged with the need to develop educational methods for "infusing inclusion as a core element of course process and design" (Ferdman 2010, 1).

The various dimensions of the more active role of ordinary individuals in constructing foreign policies worldwide could support a wider use of active teaching and learning techniques—that is, teaching methods that ask students to participate in constructing their own knowledge (Shaw 2010).

According to Jeffrey S. Lantis, Kent J. Kill, and Matthew Krain, there are five key dimensions for contemporary active teaching and learning: (1) case studies; (2) alternative texts, such as films and television, music, cartoons and political humor, novels and memoirs, and news articles and editorials; (3) simulations, games, and role-playing; (4) use of technology in the classroom; and (5) service learning (Lantis, Kill, and Krain 2010). The following section of this chapter describes an example of educational initiative based on the intersection of at least four of those dimensions of active learning.

THE UNIVERSITY OF ST. MARY (USM) EXAMPLE

For five consecutive years, undergraduate students at the University of Saint Mary (USM) in Kansas wrote scenarios for role-playing exercises (simulations) about real international or internationally relevant conflicts. Researched in the fall semester and written in the spring semester, these scenarios served as the bases for annual one-day conferences that the university hosted and conducted for area high school students. Each year, some five to seven high schools participated, bringing together approximately 120 students.

Prior to the conferences, USM student authors traveled to each high school to tutor the students on the topics and roles to be played. During the conferences, the high school students played the roles in the simulation written by the university students. The student authors of the scenarios acted as the primary hosts at the conference.

The students wrote scenarios on the following cases: genocide in Darfur (2008), Georgian–Russian conflict over North Ossetia (2009), problems between Pakistan and its breakaway region of Baluchistan (2010), historically determined problems between Turkey and Armenia (2011), differences among the positions taken on the civil conflict in Syria by the United States and European Union on the one hand and Russia and China on the other (2012), and the continuing humanitarian crisis in Darfur (2013).

For the American student, all these cases represent very different and scarcely known geopolitical and sociopsychological locations. In each case, the class was prepared through the generic discussion previously outlined, and then the topic for the conference was chosen by the participating USM students from subjects in the current news (CNN, BBC, *New York Times*, etc.) through the following process.

GOALS AND LEARNING OBJECTIVES

The overall goal of the educational initiative was, in accordance with the goals of educational simulations in IR in general, to help students to "increase their perceived understanding of other countries' position on issues, move outside the 'boundaries of their locales and experiences,' and develop greater empathy" (Butcher 2012, 177; Krain and Lantis 2006, 404). In addition, the project was aimed at helping students to deepen their "conceptual understanding of a particular phenomenon, sets of interactions, or sociopolitical processes by using student interaction to bring abstract concepts to life" (Lantis, Kille, and Krain 2010).

The learning objectives of the courses that included work on scenarios can be divided into: (1) the pedagogical or educational objectives and (2) the subject matter, or international studies objectives. Pedagogically, the project was inspired by the classical emancipatory education literature that emphasizes the pedagogy of inclusion and deconstruction of power relationship among the instructors and the students (Freire 1998; Ranciere 1991). The inspiration for the pedagogical structure of the project was provided by the ideas of Bernardo M. Ferdman about "teaching inclusion by practicing it" (2010, 39).

Accordingly, the pedagogical objectives for the students included gaining a hands-on illustration of a more egalitarian educational setting, with the idea of reducing power barriers between the students and the professor during the educational process, and gaining a hands-on illustration of an inclusive educational process.

The subject matter objectives for the students included:

1. learning the content of a specific case of international or internationally relevant conflict;
2. gaining a hands-on illustration of the constructivist theory of IR;
3. gaining a hands-on understanding of the enhanced role of ordinary individuals in current IR writ large, either through different forms of popular will expression (global democracy as a way of life) or through a more careful attention to the conditions of ordinary people (human rights regime); and
4. development of analytic and communication skills.

These learning objectives required specific forms of course organization. In particular, the first two educational objectives (the reduction of power barriers between the students and the instructor and inclusiveness) needed to be carefully attended to at all stages of the course, such as the initial preparation for scenario writing, selection of topic, study of background material, preparation of handouts for the conference, identification and preparation of the needed roles, training high school students for their roles, designing a debriefing session, and assessment.

In order to reach the objective of the power barriers reduction and the objective of inclusiveness, the scenario writing courses were as much as possible organized as egalitarian workshops rather than as traditional hierarchical classes. The instructor should make every effort to create a near-even field where students and the instructor act together toward the common goal of writing a meaningful scenario and conducting a successful conference.

For example, the instructor could give students each year the choice of the international case for the conference. Likewise, at the initial planning stage, the class may act as a working group, with the student participants rather than the instructor deciding on the timetable, identifying the tasks, and setting the deadlines for completions. The goal here is to help the students to develop a sense of ownership and pride in the project instead of restricting them to the relatively detached, traditional ways aimed at passing the class with high enough grades.

INITIAL PREPARATION FOR SCENARIO WRITING

Before the students even select a specific topic for a conference, they need to become aware and sensitive toward the pedagogical objectives of the course—that is, the requirements of inclusiveness and relative egalitarianism. Thus, at the beginning of the course in the fall semester, several class meetings were usually dedicated to discussion of relevant emancipatory education literature. Some selections from Paulo Freire's (1998) and Jacques Ranciere's (1991) works have proven helpful. Applying these theories to the course requires the establishment of ground rules for the semester.

The ground rules need to reflect the more egalitarian nature of the project, wherein the students' own perspectives, prior knowledge, and experiences are to be highly valued, with the implicit intention of giving the students a sense of ownership and pride in the final product. At the same time, the ground rules need to include a safeguard against the possibility that students would take advantage of the more egalitarian structure of the course. Thus, the ground rules should stipulate that most decisions in the course would be made by consensus; however, the rules should also state that the decisions could be overridden at the discretion of the instructor.

SELECTION OF TOPIC

Students selecting a topic may be assigned to bring one to three news articles pertaining to different international conflicts. On their assigned days, students could make classroom presentations on their chosen articles. That presentation should cover three major questions:

1. What does the article argue?
2. What is the story behind the article?
3. Why is it worthy to use as a case for the USM conference?

Next, the students write a one- to two-page paper for each case explaining why this case merited becoming the basis for an educational simulation. The directions for this paper should be kept to the minimum so that the students could continue to develop the sense of self-reliance and personal ownership of the project. There should be no restrictions on the proposal of the cases at this time. No case should be tabooed as inappropriate.

Classroom discussion may indicate that some cases are inappropriate on the basis of political sensitivities, but it is important that this decision comes from the students themselves rather than being imposed on them by the instructor. Student participants show a lot of common sense and commitment to the project and have no difficulty with the choice of an appropriate topic.

After discussing all the cases identified by the students, each class should try to reach consensus on a case. If this is impossible, then the class may proceed to a vote. At this stage of the process, the instructor should let the students' choice of topic prevail for the sake of the objectives of egalitarianism and inclusiveness, even if it appears that a different topic would be better.

STUDY OF BACKGROUND MATERIAL

After the topic of the scenario is identified, the class may turn to a study of the history of the issue and the parties involved in it. This stage is usually approached with the understanding that the final product could be only as good as the authors' knowledge of the subject. Usually a key reference book or a textbook is identified for studying the history and complexities of the chosen case, and the students then do further research into various elements and current developments of each case.

For example, Totten and Markusen's (2006) text on Darfur and Stephen Cohen's (2006) *The Idea of Pakistan* have proven helpful general introductions to their respective cases. Additionally, alternative texts, such as films (*Darfur Now* [Brown 2008], *Partition* [Sarin 2007], and *Ararat* [Egoyan 2003] were viewed in different years), news (Charlie Rose's interview on Georgia [Rose 2008]), and memoirs (Fethiye Cetin's *My Grandmother: A Memoir* [2012]), make the case more alive for the students. However, it is a challenge to find material reflecting the narratives and points of view of *both* sides of a conflict, in part because the cases are so politically laden.

For example, in the case of the United States' and Russia's disagreements on the situation in Syria, one may have to resort to the English-language editions of Russian news agencies to find alternative texts presenting views of the Russian side. To get a Turkish point of view of the historical Armenian-Turkish conflicts and current tensions, one may have to go to YouTube to find the (anti-Armenian) documentary *Armenian Revolt*. The point is that to study the narratives of both sides of a conflict, the class had to put in much effort, and technology was used intensively in the classroom as a form of active teaching and learning.

SELECTION OF ROLES

Once students adequately immerse themselves in the history and other background material, they are assigned to write analytic papers describing the case and identifying six to eight major groups involved in or touched by the conflict. From the identified groups and categories, composite characters should be developed for the role-playing scenarios. Character selection can be achieved at the end of the fall semester of the two-semester course.

The second semester of the course should have the fall research class as a prerequisite, so most students moved from the fall to the spring course. On the basis of the previously identified categories for the conflict participants created in the first semester, the second-semester students began developing and drafting roles for the scenario.

The development of the roles is a true exercise in intersectionality, as the characters are supposed to represent various identities (such as an Ossetian woman, a Baluchi terrorist, an Armenian historian, or a Russian military officer) while also having the personal appeal of real people to whom the students (including the high school students) could relate.

In order to meet the simulation's goals of increasing students' understanding of other countries' positions on issues, as well as of moving "outside the 'boundaries of their locales and experiences,' and develop greater empathy" (Butcher 2012, 177), the students are asked to try to remain true to the characters' ways of constructing their international, interethnic, or other intergroup interests and identities and also to try to imagine what the student-authors themselves would be doing, feeling, and thinking if they were to be born and raised at that place and at that time.

INTRODUCING THE INTERNATIONAL CLASSROOM FORMAT

Constructing the characters' identities as close to reality as possible is one of the hardest things to do for the students. There is always the question of realism and understanding. For example, the problem became especially difficult during the preparation for writing of the scenario for the conference in 2012, when the American students needed to realistically construct the Russian position on the Syrian conflict. In order to achieve a better understanding of it, to take the guess work out of the situation, the class established communication with university students in Russia.

This started the so-called Project WE—the virtual international classroom experiment that brought together students from USM with a class at the Institute for Russian Language in Moscow. The meeting place for the combined class was in a specially created Facebook group, thus providing a virtual international classroom space.

PROJECT WE

The purpose of this project was to help the American and Russian student participants to explore together some of the key concepts of IR. The project was based on the recognition that, without exposure to people and meanings from different countries and cultures, many students tended to "essentialize" their own understanding of concepts and to consider them natural and universal.

During the fall semester of 2011, the U.S. and Russian students were asked to explain what certain IR concepts meant to them. They explored the meanings of the concepts of power, security, conflict, peace, and freedom. The students used a photovoice version of the narrative analysis and posted pictures on Facebook illustrating how they saw a concept, along with a short explanation of their ideas. Then the student participants from the two countries engaged in dialogue about their visions of the concepts.

This proved to be an effective and low-cost way of achieving firsthand exposure to other ideas and ways of constructing one's ethical positions, as well as interests. A fuller, detailed description of this project and its implications goes beyond the limits of this chapter. Suffice it to say, this virtual classroom experience did help the USM students to understand the Russian position better and to write a more realistic simulation scenario.

Meanwhile, the international classroom format was adopted and further developed by Carolyn Shaw of Wichita State University, who has organized a number of interuniversity multicountry international classrooms (groups) on Facebook to bring the virtual international classroom exchange to a new level.

CONCLUSION

The educational projects described in this chapter clearly show the applicability and effectiveness of intersectionality-inspired teaching methods for the IR classrooms. Such methods capture the importance of the rise of the global commoner (a development in IR described in the beginning of this chapter) and acknowledge the individuality of every student in class. The students are challenged to be active participants in creating real-world scenarios and making decisions in these projects. The principles of egalitarianism, inclusiveness, and cooperation are essential for these educational projects.

Chapter Two

Intersectionality and the Spoken Word

Toward a Pedagogy Understanding of Culture

Richard S. Rawls and Janita L. Rawls

A preclass conversation with a student provided a startling realization. The conversation serves as an appropriate introduction to the entire theme of this chapter. The student had exhibited poor writing skills and an even poorer grasp of assessable events through writing. His spoken English was without an accent because his parents brought him as a two-year-old when they immigrated to the United States. What startled us was that the conversation revealed that he had grasped far more of the assigned reading and its issues than would have been apparent if he had been asked to write out his thoughts. It would have been perfectly natural to assume that the student was not diligent in his studies. Yet, as the student walked to class and talked about the day's assigned reading, he disclosed not only a thorough comprehension of the text but also a vital understanding of the book and its limitations as a primary source.

This experience raised questions about how educators assess progress, achievement of course outcomes, and attainment of classroom goals. Above all, it forced a question about what precisely the assignment assessed: writing or analytical skills? If a student with poor writing skills could demonstrate analysis through an oral assessment, then maybe the medium of assessment was not well-chosen.

College instructors face classrooms comprised not only of students from their own culture, who have varied skills and abilities in writing and speaking, but also students from around the globe. The Western, if not the Anglo-American, assumption is that students arrive prepared to write well in college classes, but as experience increasingly and sadly demonstrates, this is not always true.

Some state colleges and universities offer dozens upon dozens of remedial writing courses; others require poor writers to take remedial writing classes at a two-year school (junior college, community college, etc.); still others refuse to admit students until they *fix* their writing. Meanwhile, public secondary teachers must also teach to a diverse range of abilities in their classes. The increased internationalization of secondary and university classes means that students arrive on campus from around the world. Educational institutions frequently lose sight of the oral nature of the cultures from both within and outside their countries and of the students arriving to study.

Walter Ong observes in his famous study, *Orality and Literacy*: "Language is so overwhelmingly oral that of all the many thousands of languages—possibly tens of thousands—spoken in the course of human history only around 106 have ever been committed to writing to a degree sufficient to have produced literature, and most have never been written at all" (1988, 7). One reason for the increased use of oral assignments and assessments is the natural function of orality. Ong further notes, "By contrast with natural, oral speech, writing is completely artificial" (1988, 81).

As assessment has matured in the last three decades, evaluation instruments have been refined. Initially, a passing grade was sufficient to prove that effective learning transpired. Then, standardized tests and rubrics were developed. Regional accreditation bodies seeking to consistently measure learning required rubrics as a standard within an institution. To further add to the assessment discussion, disciplinary accreditation agencies touted the effectiveness of standardized testing to benchmark student learning. Standardized tests or written assessments, however, are not the sole assessment measures available. A variety of oral assessments exists, but their use has been seen as an afterthought to written assessment.

The term *oral assessment* is used to define any review by speaking. *Oral assessment* is formally defined by Gordon Joughin as "assessment in which a student's response to the assessment task is verbal, in the sense of being expressed or conveyed by speech instead of writing" (1998, 367). Three different forms of oral assessment exist: (1) presentations, (2) examinations, and (3) applications (Joughin n.d.). These forms allow for students at any level to share knowledge and interact with others so that a variety of skills can be assessed.

As education increasingly becomes global, educators across all disciplines must review how oral assessments *are* and *can be* used in the teaching and learning process. In areas with high numbers of second-language-speaking students, key competency evaluation becomes difficult. This remains especially evident with written assessments.

Some disciplines have in response embraced oral assessments as a primary form of learning: medicine (Simpson and Ballard 2005), law (Wallace 2010), language teaching and learning (Joughin 1998), and health sciences generally. Additionally, from a professional setting, the use of oral assessments is crucial in the hiring and promotion processes, where interviews are a standard, accepted mode of inquiry.

ESTABLISHING FAIR AND INCLUSIVE PRAXIS: PERSPECTIVES FROM ACADEMIC LITERATURE

In addition to Ong's insight into orality, a second reason for the incorporation of more oral assignments relates to writing. Some students find writing difficult because they do not grasp the rules of writing, from syntax to the proper organization of a paper. Professors, teachers, and others frequently make great efforts to help students write but with frustrating results. This failure can flow from hundreds of reasons: struggles with dyslexia, a lack of exposure to reading and writing as a toddler, growing up in a culture or family prizing oral forms of communication over written forms. These struggles should receive the concerned attention that is often devoted to them. Because, as Ong notes, "[t]alk implements conscious life but it wells up into consciousness," showing students how to deliver a carefully crafted speech might actually help them in their written endeavors (1988, 4). The appendix shows how certain oral assignments can be crafted in such a way as to also help students with the structure of written assignments.

A third justification for increased assessment through student speaking pertains to the increasingly "sound-bite" nature of American and, indeed, English-speaking societies throughout the world. Right or wrong, people are judged by how well they communicate in both written and oral forms. People judge the intelligence of others based on their capacity to communicate. In many parts of the world, jobs, promotions, admission into professional and graduate programs, and other significant events hinge on the student's ability to orally communicate.

A fourth rationale for increased attention to student speaking relates to assessment within the classroom. It has already been suggested that writing may not accurately assess student learning. No one assessment mechanism alone may measure all that students have learned, how far they have come, or how well they might have learned and or completed learning objectives (Angelo and Cross 1993). Use of more than one type of assessment measure will be far more accurate and helpful for many academic subjects than just a single assessment mechanism (Fink 2003). The ability to communicate well leads to power and enfranchisement because it helps the communicator in the eyes of others. According to Bonnie T. Dill and Ruth E. Zambrana, "[i]nterpersonal power refers to routinized, day-to-day practices of how people treat one another. Such practices are systematic, recurrent, and so familiar that they often go unnoticed" (2009, 11).

Research on diversity and inclusion provides additional reasons for oral assessments. According to Bernardo M. Ferdman, some of the in-class behaviors fostering inclusiveness include "connecting and engaging with other people; listening skillfully and deeply; being transparent, speaking up, and sharing information, as well as encouraging a broad range of others to do so" (2010, 40). His stress on "listening skillfully and deeply" is yet another benefit from forms of oral assessment that involve presenting material to a class. Students learn both from having an audience and from being an audience. The careful cultivation and encouragement of listening can therefore be anything but passive.

The intention in considering oral assessments ought to be not only a multiplicity of assessment modes but also transformation of the learner and the education process. To this end, Dill and Zambrana argue that transformation should change the learner, knowledge, and society itself: "Discussions of social change [ought to] focus not just on changing the society at large but also on changing structures of knowledge within institutions of higher learning and the relationship of colleges and universities to society" (2009, 13).

ORAL ASSESSMENTS: EFFECTS ON LEARNING

Gordon Joughin and Gillian Collom provide several reasons for testing student knowledge through oral review, including (1) authenticity, (2) promoting good learning, (3) balancing and developing student strengths, and (4) countering plagiarism (2003, 1078). They define *authenticity* as the ability of educators to practice oral communication in an educational setting that mimics a professional setting or practice. Learning is also strengthened by oral assessments because students view these forms of assessment as more personal, challenging, and engaging (Joughin and Collom 2003, 1080).

Time on task is crucial to student learning, and activities promoting engagement are invaluable to the teaching and learning process. Active oral communication is a fundamental mode of learning (Modaff and Hopper 1984). Furthermore, assessment must be accurate in capturing student knowledge. Oral assessment can balance other forms of assessment within a course or professional setting. Finally, the use of oral assessments discourages plagiarism because students remain aware that they must be prepared for a questioning period.

IMPLEMENTING ORAL EXAMINATIONS AS ASSESSED EVENTS

A model illuminating the complexity of issues involved in determining sound oral assessment praxis exists. This model, which includes the following six factors, remains vital for fair praxis as well as consistent evaluation and assessment (Joughin 1998, 368):

1. primary content type (knowledge and understanding, applied problem-solving ability, interpersonal competence, and personal qualities),
2. interaction (presentation or dialogue),
3. authenticity (contextualized or decontextualized),
4. structure (closed or open),
5. examiners (self-assessment; peer-assessment or authority-based assessment), and
6. orality (purely oral or orality as secondary).

Each factor or practice needs to be defined before the oral examination is given. First, the oral examination must have a framework to answer an important question: What are the main competencies, or primary content type, for which the oral examination will be focused? Determination of the focus guides the student in preparation. Additionally, the primary content type directs the number and composition of examiners. For example, will the oral examination be evaluated by one faculty member, two faculty members, or a range of student peers? This determination affects how a student prepares for the event and could influence the examination's outcome.

In addition to the number and kind of examiners present, care must be given to ensure that standard evaluative objectives and concepts exist between each reviewer. Each examiner must be able to articulate the required command of content. Influencing this aspect is the practice of authenticity, as examiners determine the kind of background in which to set or contextualize the oral examination. Examiners may set the oral examination within any context of professional practice.

Each reviewer must understand the amount of acceptable prompting, or interaction. In a standard written exam, one prompt is given by the question, originating with the faculty member. All students receive the same prompt with which to articulate concepts. In an oral examination, examiners must decide on the level of prompting that is acceptable to determine if the student has mastered the content and objectives.

This factor or practice, interaction, is influenced by the level of structure—that is, whether there is a closed set of questions to follow or an open structure. As Joughin points out, several studies consider structure one of the fundamental dimensions of oral assessment (1998, 372) because structure may determine the reliability of the oral assessment (Muzzin and Hart 1985; Yang and Laube 1983).

Prior to structure, the degree or level of orality present for the assessment must be understood by all examiners. A central question is this: Is the oral examination the primary vehicle for assessment, or is it a secondary mode of assessment to a written assignment?

IMPLEMENTING ORAL PRESENTATIONS AS ASSESSED EVENTS

The possibilities for assessments through oral presentations remain open to creative flexibilities. They offer engaged and integrated learning opportunities, but they also require significant thinking prior to implementation. Solid pedagogical principles should inform the design and implementation of such assessments. Listed here are both suggestions for things to consider before creating the assignments and ideas for crafting a useful educational experience.

Perhaps the most important component of a successful oral presentation is the effort the educator takes to guide the experience. In particular, the instructor must determine which goals, outcomes, and experiences the student should achieve through the assignment (Angelo and Cross 1993). It may sound simple, but the educator must also communicate these things to students.

Another consideration relates to the values or weights the instructor assigns to various parts of the assessed event. Failure to do this can cause confusion. If, for example, an instructor tells the class that conclusions to speeches are absolutely vital but does not weigh the conclusion accordingly, then students experience a contradiction. Finally, the feedback provided both to the individuals and to the entire class must be consistent, timely, and pertinent.

Other facets of learning relate more directly to the student experience, but instructors ought to weigh them in accordance with the assessed goals and outcomes. For example, the required time of the presentation affects student learning experiences. A longer speech provides students with an opportunity to present more research and to learn more content. If, on the other hand, one intention is to assess students' ability to analyze and critically use sources, then a shorter presentation puts students in the situation where they must separate the central from the peripheral. They must analyze which information is important to present and which should be cut.

Educators should question whether to assign specific topics to individual students, provide a list of topics and let students select from the list, or permit students to select their own topics. Each has its own merits. Faculty guidance in some courses can ensure a diversity of topics that might not otherwise be present if students were left to select on their own.

A final consideration involves the interplay between content, academic approach, and communication. While these remain linked, they can also be assessed separately. Faculty should guard against exclusively rewarding content unless that is their intention. L. Dee Fink observes, "The natural inclination of most faculty, given their training and disciplinary socialization, is to take a content-centered approach to learning goals" (2003, 73).

In other words, oral presentations can cause confusion for students. The instructor needs to communicate what is being assessed. For most classes in most disciplines, an ideal oral presentation would be assessed in terms of content, academic approach, and communication. An integrated approach might work best, but it requires the intentions of the instructor for an optimal learning environment.

CONCLUSION

There are several indisputable facts facing education, but one of the most important is the increasingly diverse student body. Ferdman's (2003a) encouragement to examine systemic institutional barriers to student learning serves as a reminder that instructors might unintentionally create such obstacles. This requires faculty to examine instructional design and praxis.

The old reliance on written work alone, while indisputably important, may ironically reveal a student weakness in writing without accurately measuring student acquisitions of other skills and achievement of goals. Expanding evaluation measures to include oral assessments would facilitate a clearer knowledge of skills and abilities requisite in professional contexts. It would also promote a more equitable system and possibly remove some of the barriers potentially found in a class of diverse students.

Chapter Three

The Law as the Language of Civil Rights

*Using Supreme Court Cases to Facilitate an Inclusive
Classroom Dialogue on Difference and Equality*

Michael A. Lewkowicz

Such recent events as the Black Lives Matter movement addressing U.S. police interactions with black communities and the expansion of same-sex marriage in America have brought many civil rights issues to the forefront of American politics and society, which has provided college instructors plenty of opportunities to facilitate classroom discussions of a variety of civil rights issues. However, a discussion of civil rights can bring on several risks, not the least of which is the potential for a polarized classroom, which in turn might alienate numerous students from the discussion and indeed from the class as a whole. Thus, it is incumbent on the instructor to devise an approach to discussing civil rights issues that facilitates a free and open discussion that engages students with a variety of perspectives, while doing so in an inclusive fashion.

This chapter discusses the use of notable U.S. Supreme Court cases as one such approach. By facilitating a classroom discussion on several cases that have shaped the definition and application of various civil rights in America, an instructor can explore the underlying issues at stake in those cases. In particular, the instructor can use the discussion to help students to develop a greater understanding of the connections between the outcomes of those cases and their daily lives, with the intent of bringing the class together rather than reinforcing divisions based on various identities.

IDENTITY, INTERSECTIONALITY, AND CLASSROOM
DISCUSSIONS OF CIVIL RIGHTS

Classroom discussions of civil rights issues can be uncomfortable for a variety of students, whether they belong to groups that have been (and often currently remain) targets of discrimination or to groups that are traditionally privileged in a society. To avoid the uncomfortable feelings such a discussion might generate, students may not wish to be involved in honest conversations involving gender, sexuality, race, and other identities. For example, Derald Wing Sue (2015) argues that discussions on race are often inhibited by several social protocols, including politeness. Because of a common desire by people to avoid confrontation, they often either avoid discussions of race altogether or they discuss race in a superficial fashion while avoiding some of the more controversial items, such as racism and white privilege.

Another potential problem with a classroom discussion of race is that students may be reluctant to participate, either due to concerns of how their involvement in the discussion might be perceived in light of their own race, or due to the perceived lack of utility for any such discussion. White students may be reluctant to engage in a conversation about race due to fears of appearing racist, the difficulty of confronting white privilege, or the desire to avoid personal responsibility to end racism, while black students may not engage in discussions they consider to be pointless due to their perceptions that someone who is not of their race can never truly understand their feelings (Sue 2015).

There is also concern that students' emotional reactions to a classroom dialogue on race can heighten class polarization: "When race issues are discussed in the classroom, however, they may push hot buttons in participants and evoke strong and powerful feelings that become very heated" (Sue 2015). Thus, these heated discussions may provoke anger, resentment, guilt, embarrassment, and frustration, often through unintentionally insensitive statements.

Dialogue involving sexual orientation or gender identity can also produce intense emotions, often via "microaggressions," such as heterosexist remarks, statements that implicitly endorse heteronormative culture, or expressions of tacit disapproval of the LGBTQ experience (Nadal 2013). Even if students do not intend to offend their classmates, their lack of awareness of LGBTQ issues can still lead to offensive and polarizing comments: "These students may be well-intentioned, but could damage a class discussion by accidentally fostering negative stereotypes about homosexuals" (Barr 2013).

Because of the sensitive and emotional nature of such discussions, a teacher may seek to avoid addressing sensitive topics like race. Avoidance of sensitive issues is not the appropriate strategy, as doing so merely reinforces the status quo regarding relationships between different identities, including race: "White silence and silencing by the educator or learner on racial matters expresses dominant views about the significance of race as a factor shaping lives" (Manglitz, Guy, and Merriweather 2014). An instructor must facilitate a classroom discussion that addresses various identity-based issues in a way that brings the classroom together rather than polarizes students along these very same identity categories.

One way to approach such a discussion is to go beyond mutually exclusive perceptions of identity, whereby one is perceived as either belonging to or not belonging to a single identity at a time, such as white versus nonwhite, black versus nonblack, female versus male, and gay and lesbian versus nongay and nonlesbian. This dichotomous approach to identity is often used in the classroom, in a court of law (Crenshaw 1989), and by representatives of groups that focus primarily on the interests of people belonging to specific identities (Goldberg 2009).

Such a stark portrayal of identity avoids the complex nature of identity, or more accurately *identities*, because people frequently embrace multiple identities at the same time. By utilizing a traditional approach to identity in addressing various civil rights issues in the classroom, the instructor provides an overly simplistic view of the human experience, particularly for students who embrace more than one traditionally oppressed identity, such as immigrant women and black members of the LGBTQ community. An instructor must open a discussion of civil rights in a way that embraces intersecting identities.

An intersectional approach can be particularly important when it comes to facilitating discussions within political science courses. To that end, Amy Cabrera Rasmussen argues for a broader intersectional political science pedagogy with an emphasis on four crucial features: "focusing on multiple identities, a foregrounding of power and process, transforming courses through inclusion and employing a normative commitment to equality" (2014, 103).

It is important for the instructor to address the connections between identity and power; "[p]olitical science can contribute significantly to the interdisciplinary conversation about how best to help students to best understand this concept, because studying power is a fundamental focus of our field" (Rasmussen 2014, 106–7). Thus, it is important to address not only interactions of identity and power but also intersections of identity with power. For example, a traditional way of discussing women in Congress is to highlight how several congresswomen have promoted traditionally feminist issues, such as equal pay and prochoice policies when it comes to abortion. However, it is inaccurate to say that all women in Congress agree on those issues, for their political views are likely to be shaped not only by gender but also their political parties, their ideologies, and their districts, as well as their other identities, which can include race, sexual orientation, gender identity, and religion. Thus, any classroom discussion of gender in Congress must acknowledge the variety of external and intrinsic influences on the political views and behaviors of its members.

DISCUSSING IDENTITIES AND SUPREME COURT CASES

An intersectional approach to civil rights can be particularly daunting when discussing relevant Supreme Court cases, which often address a single dimension of identity at a time. When asked to rule on civil rights issues, Supreme Court justices are asked to clarify the constitutional status of laws that affect members of traditionally oppressed identities, such as nonwhite people, women, or the LGBTQ community. Furthermore, when members of the Supreme Court use their power to promote equality for members of traditionally oppressed identities, their rulings often have consequences that affect not only those people from identities that directly benefit from the ruling but also those people from other identities for whom the consequences are indirect, not to mention the broader consequences on society as a whole.

One such indirect consequence might be increased polarization between members of different groups (embracing different identities) along a single dimension. In theory, some members of traditionally privileged groups might feel empathy toward those people from historically oppressed groups. However, if they do not recognize the ruling as relevant to their own daily lives, then they might support the ruling in principle but may not fully get behind it in practice, particularly if the ruling might disrupt their previously privileged status. Some members of traditionally privileged groups may consistently view civil rights as a zero-sum game, whereby a policy change, such as a Supreme Court decision, that benefits one traditionally oppressed group will result in losses for their group and vice versa. Thus, they will certainly oppose any Supreme Court decision that they perceive will impose costs upon them.

The legalization of same-sex marriage across the United States is a perfect example of this dynamic, as the ruling in *Obergefell v. Hodges* (576 U.S. __, 135 S. Ct. 2584 [2015]) was intended to promote marriage equality. However, that decision provoked a backlash among religious conservatives, including those who were concerned that implementation of the decision may lead some people to be forced to either violate their religious convictions or to risk losing their jobs.

The Supreme Court decision in *Obergefell* provided excellent fodder for a classroom discussion, as that decision resulted in tangible, salient consequences, not only for same-sex couples but also for members of other identities, particularly religious conservatives. Thus, opening a classroom dialogue on this case provides an opportunity to address a variety of potential consequences of the ruling on numerous identities.

ELEMENTS TO A DISCUSSION OF CIVIL RIGHTS CASES

This approach relies largely on the traditional case-study method, whereby students are encouraged to learn about the background of a civil rights case, the key legal principles established by the Supreme Court decision, and the significance of this case on the U.S. Constitution (Leming 1991). However, unlike the use of case studies, this approach focuses on not only the direct consequences of the case for those from groups who benefit from the decision but also on the indirect consequences for those from other groups as well as for society as a whole.

BACKGROUND

At the outset of the discussion of each Supreme Court case, the instructor should facilitate a classroom discussion of the circumstances that led up to that case. In addition to addressing the events surrounding the case, it is crucial for the class to address noteworthy legal issues at stake in the case, with an emphasis on legal arguments put forth by both sides of the case. Encouraging students to discuss the legal arguments (as opposed to political or pragmatic arguments) not only helps students to understand the arguments and issues involved in the case but also should hopefully temper the emotional reactions that the more political and pragmatic arguments might elicit.

SUPREME COURT DECISION

This discussion should address the key legal principles that were established or reaffirmed by a Supreme Court ruling, with an emphasis on how the justices rooted those principles in an analysis of the U.S. Constitution. Through such an analysis, students can gain an understanding of the legal and constitutional framework of their rights, as well as potential limitations to those rights. If time permits, it is also useful to discuss noteworthy concurring and dissenting opinions so that students can examine multiple legal perspectives on those rights.

When addressing civil rights, much of the discussion of fundamental legal principles is likely to revolve around how Supreme Court justices have interpreted the "due process" and "equal protection" clauses of the U.S. Constitution. In particular, the "due process" clause ensures that governments cannot deprive someone of "life, liberty, or property, without due process of law." Established by the Fifth Amendment in 1791, this guarantee originally only applied to the federal government, but it was extended to state governments via the Fourteenth Amendment in 1868.

The Fourteenth Amendment also includes the "equal protection" clause, which ensures that states do not "deny to any person within its jurisdiction the equal protection of the laws." Along with the "due process" clause, this clause has provided much of the foundation for Supreme Court decisions extending constitutional protections to the black community, women, the LGBTQ community, and other identities.

CONSEQUENCES

This discussion addresses the various direct and indirect consequences of a Supreme Court decision. A discussion of direct consequences typically focuses on those outcomes that benefitted or harmed members of a specific identity that is the direct focus of the case. A discussion of indirect consequences addresses those consequences that might affect members of other identities or society as a whole, which in turn should generate a more inclusive (as opposed to divisive) discussion.

For example, in *Shelby County v. Holder* (570 U.S. __, 133 S. Ct. 2612 [2013]), the Supreme Court examined the 1965 Voting Rights Act, which required that the U.S. attorney general or a three-judge panel from the U.S. District Court of District of Columbia preclear any changes to election law made by state or local governments with a history of racial discrimination, so as to ensure that those changes did not have a discriminatory impact. Although the Supreme Court upheld the preclearance provision, it struck down the formula used to determine which governments had a history of discrimination on the basis that the formula was based on data from 1972 and thus irrelevant to current conditions. As a result, the preclearance provision would be rendered unenforceable until Congress developed a new formula. This decision paved the way for states to pass election laws resulting in racial discrimination, as enforcement would not be until after the fact.

A discussion of the direct consequences of this case highlights those election changes that have the most potential to discriminate against racial minorities, such as racial gerrymandering. Without a preclearance provision, legislators seeking to reduce the power of black voters can redraw legislative districts in a way that packs as many black voters into as few districts as possible. By concentrating their representation into a small geographic area, this legislative map would reduce the influence of black voters throughout the state.

Although racially unbalanced redistricting maps may eventually be stricken down by the courts, the decision in *Shelby County v. Holder* ensures that any changes to these maps would not be undertaken until after someone has brought the issue to the courts. Thus, those racially unbalanced maps are likely to exist for one or more election cycles, depending on how long it takes for the courts to resolve the legal issues, not to mention the ultimate outcome of those ensuing cases.

The class can also discuss the indirect consequences of *Shelby County v. Holder* by addressing those election changes that not only discriminate against racial minorities but other groups as well, such as laws that limit the types of documents voters can use to prove their identities before being allowed to vote. Some people argue that requiring voters to show specific forms of voter identification, such as a driver's license, a passport, or another type of government-issued identification, can disproportionately affect black voters, who are less likely to have the specific types of required identification (General Accounting Office 2014).

However, such requirements might also disenfranchise the poor, the elderly, and college-age students, particularly those out-of-state students who might not have a driver's license for the state in which they reside during the election. By facilitating a discussion of disenfranchisement of a variety of identities (not just racial), the instructor can then elaborate on the impact of these rulings, not only on certain groups of voters, but also on election outcomes and ensuing policies.

LAYING THE GROUNDWORK FOR THE
CLASSROOM DISCUSSION

In order to facilitate the best possible discussion, it is useful to prime students with an assignment in which they address several of the aforementioned elements of the Supreme Court cases (background, decisions, direct and indirect consequences). Given the complexity of some of these cases and the amount of research needed for the assignment to be worthwhile in facilitating a good discussion, a short homework assignment is ideal for a survey course, such as American Government. In some respects, this assignment is similar to a case briefing used in constitutional law courses, albeit a bit longer (two to four pages). Both approaches ask students to discuss the background and the ruling of the Supreme Court. However, whereas a case briefing is focused largely on the legal principles established by the Supreme Court decision, this assignment emphasizes the direct and indirect consequences of that decision.

To provide a focus for the discussion, students are given a list of cases from which to choose, with at least one case for each of the identities to be addressed by the course. Students are given the opportunity to sign up for the cases of their choosing several weeks in advance of the due date. There is a limit to the number of students allowed to sign up for analyzing and discussing a particular case, so as to ensure that each case has a sufficient number of informed students who could start a vibrant classroom discussion.

Using Supreme Court cases to address civil rights issues in survey courses in American Government has been a regular practice of mine for many years. The fall 2015 semester at Georgia Gwinnett College, an open-access higher education institution just outside of Atlanta with a diverse student body, was no exception. Among the cases addressed during the fall semester were *Brown v. Board of Education* (347 U.S. 483 [1954]), which ended racial segregation in public schools; *United States v. Virginia* (518 U.S. 515 [1996]), which opened the Virginia Military Academy to women; and *Obergefell v. Hodges* (576 U.S. __, 135 S. Ct. 2584 [2015]), which required states to provide marriage licenses to same-sex couples, as well as to recognize same-sex marriage licenses from other states.

DISCUSSING RACE: *BROWN V. BOARD OF EDUCATION*

In 1954, the U.S. Supreme Court ruled in favor of thirteen black families in Topeka, Kansas, who sought to enroll their children in an all-white school. Their decision in *Brown v. Board of Education* overturned the "separate but equal" principle established in *Plessy v. Ferguson* (163 U.S. 537 [1896]), which allowed for segregation of public facilities, provided those facilities were approximately equal in quality. Delivering the opinion for the unanimous court, Chief Justice Earl Warren stated, "[I]n the field of public education, the doctrine of 'separate but equal' has no place. Separate educational facilities are inherently unequal." By overturning the precedent established in *Plessy v. Ferguson*, the Supreme Court paved the way for the end of segregation, not only for educational facilities but also for all public facilities.

In one respect, facilitating a discussion of racial issues with *Brown v. Board of Education* was somewhat easy due to at least moderate levels of student familiarity with the outcome of the case, as well as their eagerness to discuss this case. For example, during the fall 2015 sign-up period two weeks prior to the American Government classes' discussion of these cases, *Brown v. Board of Education* was one of the first cases to reach the maximum number of students, thus indicating a certain level of interest in (or at least familiarity with) the case. Furthermore, facilitating a classroom discussion of the direct consequences of the case was effortless, largely because a substantial number of students at this diverse institution would likely have not made it to college if *Brown v. Board of Education* had not established the principle of integration of public schools. Many black and Latino students were willing to offer up their presence at Georgia Gwinnett College as a direct consequence of *Brown v. Board of Education* during the classroom discussion.

That is not to say that using *Brown v. Board of Education* for the classroom discussion was not without its challenges. A key challenge was in trying to get students to consider the broader impact of the case, such as the increasing diversity of American society, not just in the classroom, but also in the job market, the real estate market, and the supermarket, among many other places. Students were able to recognize that they or their classmates would not necessarily have been in the classroom if not for *Brown v. Board of Education*. However, they did not necessarily recognize that the impact of that decision went further than just the classroom; their families might not have lived in the extremely diverse Gwinnett County if not for employment and educational opportunities over the past sixty years. The diversity of the school and the county is something that many of today's generation often take for granted, but it would not have been possible without *Brown v. Board of Education*.

In addressing this case, it was vital that students not only acknowledge the diversity of the classroom (and indeed of society as a whole), but they also needed to understand the value of diversity. To that end, the outcome of the classroom discussion was mixed, as students typically volunteered their acknowledgment of the diverse classroom, while requiring additional discussion to facilitate their understanding of how a classroom and indeed a society as a whole benefit from the inclusion of a variety of ideas and viewpoints, which can be particularly important in an increasingly global society.

DISCUSSING GENDER: *UNITED STATES V. VIRGINIA*

Until 1996, the Virginia Military Academy (VMI) was the last remaining exclusively male public higher education institution. The VMI provided rigorous training and preparation for military leadership and excluded women from admissions. The U.S. government brought a federal lawsuit against the VMI and the state of Virginia, seeking to end that institution's practice of excluding women. After the U.S. Fourth Circuit Court ruled against the VMI, the state of Virginia proposed a parallel program, the Virginia Women's Institute for Leadership, to be located at Mary Baldwin College, a private liberal arts college. In a 7–1 decision, the Supreme Court ruled against the state of Virginia, with Justice Ruth Bader Ginsburg delivering the majority opinion, which stated that the parallel program proposal was insufficient to ensure equality for women: "Virginia has closed this facility to its daughters and, instead, has devised for them a 'parallel program,' with a faculty less impressively credentialed and less well paid, more limited course offerings, fewer opportunities for military training and for scientific specialization."

Beyond the immediate impact of this decision on the admission of women to the Virginia Military Institute, the decision also sent a symbolic message as to the potential importance of women for the military that served as a starting point for the American Government course discussion on the Supreme Court ruling, as students (particularly female students) volunteered their thoughts on the impact the ruling had on women in military combat and leadership roles. With some additional prodding by the instructor, students also addressed the implications of women in military leadership roles on the treatment of women in the military. To that end, several students offered thoughts as to whether the increase in the number of women in key military leadership positions would result in change in the official response of the military leadership to allegations of sexual harassment and assault.

Another item of discussion was the potential of women being drafted into military service. It took some additional questioning for students to consider the military draft as an issue for debate, but once the issue was in the open, students engaged in a lively debate about whether eligibility for a military draft should be equal on the basis of gender, a debate that shed light on an often-overlooked aspect of gender equality. Whereas traditional discussions of gender equality often revolve around purely beneficial outcomes for women, such as ensuring equal access to jobs or equal pay, this discussion highlighted the potential for gender equality eliminating traditional protections for women, such as their ineligibility for the military draft.

DISCUSSION OF SEXUAL IDENTITY: *OBERGEFELL V. HODGES*

In *United States v. Windsor* (570 U.S. 12 [2013]), the Supreme Court ruled that the federal government must recognize same-sex marriages. Two years later, the court extended that recognition by requiring that state governments not only recognize same-sex marriages from other states but also issue same-sex marriage licenses. Writing for the 5–4 majority, Justice Anthony Kennedy stated, "The right to marry is a fundamental right inherent in the liberty of the person, and under the Due Process and Equal Protection Clauses of the Fourteenth Amendment couples of the same-sex may not be deprived of that right and that liberty."

One aspect of the case that made the discussion of the indirect consequences of the ruling both easier and more challenging was the controversy surrounding the implementation of the Supreme Court's decision. In September 2015, Rowan County, Kentucky, clerk Kim Davis refused to issue marriage licenses to same-sex couples, saying that doing so would violate her religious beliefs. As a result, she was held in contempt of federal court and was subsequently jailed for several days. Because the controversy surrounding the Kentucky clerk's actions and incarceration received a great deal of media attention just weeks before the classroom discussion, its timeliness likely primed students to think about the potential effects of same-sex marriage on religious conservatives. Thus, several students volunteered a description of not only Kim Davis's actions but also other scenarios that could (and did) produce similar tensions (e.g., wedding cakes, floral arrangements, wedding photo sessions) between religious conservatives and same-sex couples seeking to get married.

Where the discussion became more challenging was in getting a variety of students to volunteer their thoughts about the issue beyond simply describing the facts. None of the students argued that the court went too far in citing Kim Davis for contempt of court. One explanation for the lack of support for Kim Davis's position could have been that the classroom was mostly comprised of students from the millennial generation, which is largely supportive of same-sex marriage, and thus there was no one in the class who agreed with Kim Davis's actions. However, another explanation is that, given the strong support the millennial generation has for same-sex relationships, students who shared Kim Davis's religious convictions (or at least the principle of religious liberty) and thus supported her actions may not have openly stated their support for fear of appearing intolerant to their classmates.

CONCLUSION

The language of civil rights is often the language of the law. In other words, to understand civil rights issues in America, it is important to understand how the courts (particularly the U.S. Supreme Court) have interpreted those issues over the years. Furthermore, by incorporating Supreme Court decisions in a discussion of civil rights and the Supreme Court, an instructor can ideally facilitate an inclusive discussion that minimizes classroom polarization.

In doing so, this chapter builds up the approaches that others have taken in teaching constitutional law, particularly in the emphasis on the use of a case's historical context advocated by the Institute of Education Sciences: "Teach Supreme Court cases in historical context so that the constitutional issue is cast within the social forces that generated it. . . . By discussing the legal precedents to a modern decision, students can begin to understand both the continuity and fluidity of the law, as well as the political and social times in which a case is decided" (Leming 1991).

This historical context can be particularly important in helping students to recognize how different identities have become salient at different times. For example, discussions of the civil rights movement of the 1950s and 1960s are impossible without addressing how that movement facilitated the environment surrounding *Brown v. Board of Education*, whereby the Supreme Court came to a unanimous decision that rejected segregation, which in turn galvanized that movement even further, to the point where racial integration of public life is something that most take for granted.

In addition to incorporating various identities into a discussion of the historical context of case law, this chapter also builds on the case-study approach that is used to facilitate student involvement in the discussions.

Whereas traditional case studies often focus on the legal facts, background, and ruling of the case, as well as the significance of the case on constitutional law (Leming 1991; Power 2012), this approach focuses on the direct and indirect consequences of the case for various identity groups, as well as for American society as a whole.

The selection of cases continues to be particularly important, not only to generate discussion but also to do so in a way that the discussion remains inclusive rather than polarizing. For example, the issue of same-sex marriage was particularly salient in fall 2015 and thus generated plenty of interest, if not necessarily a wide array of opinions, either because of widespread student support of same-sex relationships or because of the desire to adhere to the millennial generation's norms in support of same-sex relationships.

However, given that the class focused on two Supreme Court cases that addressed same-sex marriage, it would be useful to also facilitate a discussion of a Supreme Court case that addressed a different LGBTQ issue. One such case might be *Lawrence v. Texas* (539 U.S. 558 [2003]), in which the Supreme Court struck down a Texas ban on sodomy between same-sex couples as a violation of the due process clause found in the Fourteenth Amendment. Unlike *Obergefell v. Hodges*, the ruling in *Lawrence v. Texas* does not directly challenge the principles of religious liberty and thus perhaps is less likely to be polarizing.

Furthermore, with its focus on the due process clause, *Lawrence v. Texas* has broader implications on the right to privacy, not only for same-sex couples, but for heterosexual couples as well. Thus, an instructor could facilitate a discussion that addresses the extent to which governments can regulate sexual behavior between consenting adults. This is a discussion that could generate a great deal of interest, but the instructor must take great care to ensure that the explicitness of the discussion is appropriate for the venue.

In closing, using Supreme Court cases is an appropriate starting point in facilitating a discussion of civil rights issues, as students are able to address the direct and indirect consequences of these cases in an inclusive fashion. However, the success of the discussion in regard to achieving those aims will depend on the selection of the cases, as well as the ability of the instructor to direct the discussion in a way that gets students to consider the indirect consequences of those cases.

Chapter Four

Applying Insights from the Literature on Intersectionality to Teaching Political Science

Dovilė Budrytė

Amy Cabrera Rasmussen (2014) articulates the main tenets of an intersectional pedagogy in political science. She argues that this concept is essential for the discipline to adapt to the new demographic and social realities in the United States. Developing an intersectional pedagogy includes learning to appreciate multiple identities, understanding the processes related to power, transforming what we teach through the inclusion of diverse experiences, and committing to equality. This chapter contributes to these emerging attempts in political science and related disciplines to develop intersectional pedagogies that can be used for teaching in diverse classrooms. It starts out by defining the term itself, then moves on to a description of promising intersectional pedagogies, and finally describes three specific class activities. This chapter argues that intersectional pedagogies can be enriched by using concepts from trauma education, which encourages the appropriate use of comparisons between traumatic collective experiences and thus helps to transcend national and ethnic identities.

INTERSECTIONALITY: THE TERM AND ITS USES

Kimberlé Crenshaw (1989) is commonly considered to be the pioneer of the intersectionality movement that radically transformed feminism. She argues that it is necessary to look into multiple systems of oppression and the intersections of various identities, such as race, gender, and class. Crenshaw draws on the specific socioeconomic situation of black women, whose concerns and experiences were very different from white women in the United States.

Examining the methodological approaches used in the studies of intersectionality is a good starting point for the development of a sound intersectional pedagogy in political science and related disciplines. These approaches fall into three categories (McCall 2009, 50–51). The first approach, anticategorical complexity, rejects and deconstructs rigid categories to capture the complexity of social life and avoid the re-creation of new inequalities. This approach is useful when deconstructing simplistic divisions into "us" and "them" and can be used to study ethnic politics, migration, terrorism, and similar topics.

The second approach, intracategorical complexity, also problematizes various boundaries and boundary-making. It focuses attention on various groups whose experiences challenge traditional thinking about these groups. For example, black feminists and feminists in the "developing" world argue that their experiences do not fit into the feminist narrative about gender relations that was developed in the West. This way of thinking does not reject the use of categories in politics and social science but suggests that it is necessary to think about the intersections that result from belonging to different groups.

The third approach, intercategorical complexity, focuses on the relationships of inequality among social groups and maps out the configurations of inequality and their causes. This approach facilitates the identification of different patterns of racial, gender, and class inequality across different regions. Thus, for example, one city can exhibit relatively low levels of class and racial wage inequality among employed men but higher gender wage inequality and class inequality among employed women. Another city may exhibit the opposite structure of inequality, where class and racial inequality, not gender inequality, matter most.

TOWARD AN INTERSECTIONAL PEDAGOGY IN POLITICAL SCIENCE

Intersectional pedagogies are widely used in various disciplines, especially women's studies, cultural studies, and sociology, to mention just a few. For example, applying an intersectional approach to community experiences of violence may be eye-opening. Focusing on the intersections of gender and ethnicity within the same community may yield very different results from focusing on just one gender or one ethnic group.

Traditionally, political science and related disciplines, such as international relations; have focused on the study of politics (following a traditional definition by Harold D. Laswell [1936]: "who gets what, when, how"); the processes related to power; government policies; and various political processes, such as elections. Intersectional approaches can enrich the study of even "traditional" topics in this field of study, such as the impact of government policies and attempts by various groups to increase their power.

The three methodological approaches outlined in the previous section suggest several principles for an intersectional pedagogy in political science. First, identities are complex, and divisions into "us" and "them" must be challenged. Second, it is important to remember that individuals can belong to several, or even many, groups at the same time. This is especially important when thinking about citizenship and human rights. Keeping multiple belongings in mind is essential for the concept of global citizenship.

Third, the study of power remains an essential concept for the study of politics. Instead of merely focusing on "who gets what, when, how," it is essential to understand how power is experienced by people belonging to different groups and how different power configurations can be seen as oppressive by one group but liberating by another. This can be especially true in postcolonial settings, when newly (re)created states develop their minority policies.

Attempts to develop an intersectional pedagogy are based on the need to find ways to avoid crude and simplistic identity politics in the classroom (including the use of *us* and *them*), learn about the shared vulnerability and interdependence of human beings, and learn how to shift perspectives (get into someone else's skin) to understand the impacts of power.

"THE UNBEARABLE WHITENESS OF BEING"

These broad principles of intersectional pedagogy can be applied to class activities. One of the main goals of the first activity is to inspire students to think about various intersections between identities and capitalism. It can be used in lower-level political science courses that cover such topics as economic liberalism, migration, racial identities, or entrepreneurship, and upper-level courses that discuss such topics as social and political integration, individual decision-making, or ethnicity. It can be adjusted to high school classrooms as well.

This activity is based on the use of "The Unbearable Whiteness of Being" (2007), a brief documentary produced by the Scottish Documentary Institute. This documentary is available online; it is only ten minutes long, and it is an excellent introduction to Asian skin lightening and related industries. A quick Google search using this term reveals many entries for various products and descriptions of how it can be done and why. For example, a commercial website about the Asian skin-lightening market explains that the reasons people with dark skin living in Asia might want to lighten their skin include a desire to appear young and to be "associated with high society" (McDougall 2015).

The documentary is a story about an ambitious small company that tries to develop a product to lighten skin and in their own words "help people to be more successful." A "good" result is lighter skin and the success in the global economy that comes with it. The documentary is full of powerful images and stories told by individuals who want to "make it" in the global economy, no matter what it takes. It is a good starting point for a class discussion about the category of "whiteness" and the meanings associated with it that are perpetuated in different cultural and political contexts.

The discussion following the documentary can include various activities, depending on the course and other factors. It could include one-minute in-class essays, group discussions, or a discussion involving the whole class. I used this documentary to discuss the concept of belonging and related theories in an upper-level course on nationalism and in survey courses on current global issues. The discussion could focus on complicated issues, such as the intersection of age, race, gender, and socioeconomic class in global economies, but it may be useful to start with a simpler, open-ended discussion focusing on student reactions.

The initial student reactions are likely to be emotional, reacting to what they see as various forms of injustice. Situational factors, such as the demographics of the student body and the institutional culture, influence the students' responses. I have used these activities at an inclusive state college that prides itself on having the most diverse student body in the southern United States. Almost every class includes students belonging to various ethnic groups, recent immigrants, veterans, and first-generation college students.

Here are a few examples of initial student reactions:

> "My reaction was slightly sad. The culture should support self-confidence with whatever skin tone one is born with."
>
> "I really think that people who are influenced by what the media is portraying (being whiter and superior) need to reeducate themselves and challenge such stupid assumptions."
>
> "They fully believe that they do not have a choice on being born the skin color they are, which is of a darker tone."

Even these initial reactions suggest that the students started to think about such issues as equality, the construction of unequal global systems, and their relationships to race, as well as the mechanisms whereby racial inequalities are perpetuated. This line of thinking was consistent with the two principles of an intersectional pedagogy articulated by Rasmussen, namely, a "fuller understanding of the processes related to acquiring and exercising power" and creating a "normative commitment to equality" (2014, 103).

My goal was to go beyond these initial reactions; therefore, the discussion about the construction of identity was linked to theories in the literature on nationalism that focus on the process of identity construction, the treatment of national identity as "primordial," and the creation of symbols associated with identity politics. This line of teaching was consistent with the anticategorical complexity approach outlined in the previous section, which encourages scrutiny and deconstruction of well-established categories. In addition, asking why many people buy similar products is a way to make the first step toward learning to shift a frame of reference.

"The Unbearable Whiteness of Being" tells a story. As such, it can prompt other stories in the classroom (as storytelling often does), some of which may focus on the experiences of groups that are usually not considered to be disadvantaged. For example, students can point out the economic misfortunes of poor whites in such places as the United States and Europe. Such stories offer useful opportunities to introduce the third, or intercategorical complexity, approach in the study of intersectionality.

STORYTELLING AND THE TEACHING OF POLITICAL SCIENCE

Unfortunately, discussions about teaching political science and related disciplines rarely include conversations about the uses of storytelling and biographies in class. These methods can be used effectively to enrich the study of potentially controversial topics, such as undocumented migration or civil rights, thus helping students to understand the complexity of identities instead of presenting a simplified "us versus them" picture.

If used properly, life stories, including the life story of an instructor, can help to create a sense of community in the classroom. I am originally from Lithuania, and I use the story of Lithuanian immigrants told by Upton Sinclair in his novel *The Jungle* (1906) to make the case that immigrants are "real" Americans and that their experiences have had an important effect on legislation in the United States. (The description of unsanitary conditions in the meat-packing industry in *The Jungle* served as an impetus for the Pure Foods and Drugs Act of 1906.)

Being able to relate individual stories to the topics pertinent to the study of the government can help to achieve one of the main goals of intersectional pedagogy, or the inclusion of diverse perspectives. In addition, individual stories challenge stereotypes, help students to deconstruct the category of "others," and help them to develop a more nuanced understanding of civil rights.

Before integrating storytelling into introductory survey political science courses, I often dreaded discussing immigration in my classes. Often this topic provoked polarized discussions in which immigrants were described as "others." Getting familiarized with intersectional pedagogy helped me to conceptualize a teaching strategy that focuses on individual life stories and storytelling.

Civil rights is an important section of courses focusing on American government and American politics. This is an opportunity to discuss the contributions of various ethnic and cultural groups to American government and politics. When teaching this section, I introduce my students to the fascinating story of Sylvia Mendez, whose parents (her father was from Mexico, her mother was from Puerto Rico) fought for her right to be educated in a white school in California when schools there were still segregated (U.S. Courts n.d.). Sylvia's story is captivating: Her family moved onto a ranch that had previously been inhabited by another group that had experienced discrimination because of their ethnicity—Japanese Americans. (Because of hysteria about spying and potential sabotage during World War II, President Roosevelt issued an executive order that forced Japanese Americans into internment camps.) Successful in agriculture, Sylvia's parents were able to achieve their dream, winning through a legal process the right for their daughter to get a better education. This case became an inspiration for the U.S. Supreme Court case *Brown v. Board of Education* that most students are already familiar with.

Analyzing the story of Sylvia Mendez is a way for both students and professors to think about political empowerment. Most importantly, it helps to show similarities between the struggles that various groups had to undertake to achieve equal treatment. Focusing on individuals and engaging in storytelling invites stories from the students and makes the case that individuals can make a difference.

Various activities, including one-minute papers, group projects, brief analytical essays, and small-group discussions can be used to incorporate individual stories in the teaching of political science. Usually few students are familiar with Sylvia Mendez's story. Often they express surprise that there was a precedent to *Brown v. Board of Education*, which helps to open discussions about other groups and issues, such as individuals with disabilities, LGBTQ rights, and women's rights.

Individual stories are ways to learn how inequalities and oppressions are experienced by "real" people and which strategies can be used to overcome these inequalities. There are many useful and easily accessible sources, such as StoryCorps or the National Public Radio (NPR) program *Code Switch*, that can help instructors to prepare lessons on politics and government with elements of storytelling in them (NPR n.d.). StoryCorps includes many accounts by recent immigrants to the United States (StoryCorps n.d.).

MULTIDIRECTIONAL MEMORY AND TEACHING POLITICAL SCIENCE

Stories about immigration and civil rights include accounts of political traumas, such as political oppression, forced migration, or even politically inspired violence. Discrimination results in multiple "mini" traumas that can occur frequently. These observations raise important questions about teaching political science in diverse classrooms: How can the presence of these traumas in our classrooms be addressed? How can teaching about various traumas be designed so that it leads to learning that is "emotionally, politically and critically significant," not shallow and sentimental (Zembylas 2008, 1)?

Drawing on insights from trauma education in the social sciences, this chapter incorporates the concept of multidirectional memory into the teaching of civil rights in political science classes. The concept of multidirectional memory was developed in literary studies by Michael Rothberg (2001), who argues that even very different experiences, such as the Holocaust and the oppression experienced by the black community, do not need to be in competition with each other. Various experiences of historical traumas can be a source of empathy, not competition.

This approach is consistent with one of the main insights about trauma education articulated by Katherine Bischoping. To avoid the burnout and compassion fatigue often experienced by instructors who teach about traumatic issues, Bischoping (2004) suggests including appropriate comparisons when teaching about genocides. She reaches this conclusion by drawing on clinical psychology, which welcomes appropriate comparisons among different traumas and acknowledges that traumas can be experienced vicariously (e.g., listening to testimonies).

Appropriate comparisons can be a powerful teaching tool in political science classes that cover such issues as civil rights and human rights. Sylvia Mendez's story can be presented by highlighting the common experiences and common memories of various groups who fought for the right to an education. W. E. B. Du Bois's essay "The Negro and the Warsaw Ghetto" (1952) can play a similar function by introducing students to the transnational memory of the Holocaust. "The Negro and the Warsaw Ghetto" can be an excellent supplementary reading in various political science classes, including American government. In this text, Du Bois describes his experience traveling to Europe during World War II and observing the oppression experienced by European Jews. Using Du Bois's text in political science classes can help to internationalize the study of civil rights by empowering students to learn about Eastern Europe and revealing appropriate connections between the Holocaust and other traumas.

Various techniques can be used to achieve these goals, including directed reading in class (or out of class), small-group discussions, and group presentations. "The Negro and the Warsaw Ghetto" is a relatively short essay, but it is a great start to introduce the concepts of shared vulnerability and human rights, thus transcending national borders when teaching political science.

CONCLUSION

In the end, one of the most important promises of intersectional pedagogies for political science may be their mandate to rethink many categories that often are used without much hesitation by political scientists. They include "national government," "national interest," and "we." The anticategorical complexity approach demands that similar categories be subjected to scrutiny to find out who is included and who is excluded from such categories.

In addition to disaggregating the categories of race, ethnic belonging, and gender, the literature on intersectionality has a lot to offer educators who are looking for pedagogical approaches that foster a nuanced understanding of controversial political issues. Instead of making generalizations about groups (e.g., "women," "nations," etc.), it is useful to think about (and inspire the students to do the same) how the complexity and individuality of the people involved in policies and political processes can be acknowledged. This approach helps to avoid negative (or positive) associations with groups of people that can have negative consequences.

The assignments presented in this chapter demonstrate the importance of complexity and individuality in the study of political processes. The study of globalization includes not only the analysis of macrofactors (such as the impact of international trade) but also the intersection of economic (dis)empowerment and race in real people's lives. The civil rights movement in the United States can be enriched by using the oral testimonies of participants in this movement and students' own stories. The international dimension of this movement can be highlighted by using the biographies and travel stories of prominent individuals, such as W. E. B. Du Bois.

Intersectional pedagogies in political science and related disciplines are in their infancy. However, even this brief chapter suggests that such pedagogies may help to transform our classrooms into spaces where the diverse experiences of students and instructors are a source of learning about power and government, where storytelling and biographies are respected sources of learning, and where cross-cultural affiliations are actively sought and respected.

ACKNOWLEDGMENTS

I would like to express special thanks to Vilana Pilinkaitė-Sotirovič for her insightful comments on the first draft of this chapter, which was written in 2009. Subsequent drafts were presented at various conferences and as a University System of Georgia Faculty Development webinar in April 2016. This webinar is available at https://www.youtube.com/watch?v=b53tkXUmI3A&feature=youtu.be.

Thanks to Ian Peddie, Jelena Subotic, Sabine Hirschauer, Natalya Riegg, Douglas Becker, and others for their comments during the webinar.

Chapter Five

Lessons from the Salad Bowl

*Contextualized Foreign Language Instruction in a
Diverse Institution*

Kristina Watkins Mormino

The speaker concluded her excellent talk on foreign language pedagogy. Her theme was inspiring and persuasive: The best way to teach students to communicate in a foreign language is to have them put new skills and vocabulary to use in meaningful contexts. Rather than emphasizing the formal aspects of the language with nonsensical drills and exercises, the teacher should create situations that require students to use the language in "natural" ways. Context is key to communication.

The speaker was asked: "Do you have any advice for dealing with a diversity of cultural perspectives? For example, a black student may understand a contextual cue differently than a white student in the same classroom, just because they belong to different subcultures. What do we do if the context is not understood in the same way by everyone?" She replied: "If African Americans see things differently than Americans, you can't concern yourself with that."

The most intriguing aspect of this comment is the Freudian slip that opposes "African Americans" with "Americans," as if the former were exterior to the latter and not a subset thereof. "Americans" are those who monolithically understand the context presented by the instructor in the proper way. They presumably constitute the majority in the class, and it is only with their correct perception that we are to concern ourselves. "African Americans," the minority other, are excluded from the learning community insofar as they fail to understand the presented context properly.

Nonetheless, to some extent the speaker was correct. Foreign language courses do build oral and written communication skills much more effectively when students use the language to *do* something. But as the United States grows both more diverse and (arguably) more accepting of diversity of all kinds, it becomes decreasingly likely that, in a given class, there will be a uniformity of understanding among students. It is imperative to dispense with the myth that students will or should understand contexts created for instruction in the same way. This chapter outlines the importance and pitfalls of context-based learning in the foreign language classroom and discusses how the values of respect, curiosity, and critical thinking should be infused into any course in which diverse learners study unfamiliar cultures.

THE IMPORTANCE OF CONTEXT

As Alice Omaggio Hadley argues, "second language programs should provide students with ample opportunities to (1) learn language in context and (2) apply their knowledge to coping with authentic language-use situations" (1993, 125). Even if the context is merely hypothetical or imagined, such as making hotel reservations, planning a dinner party, or giving the police a description of a pickpocket, a plausible scenario facilitates language comprehension and production and provides an excellent platform for teaching culture.

Despite the meshing of language and culture in the goal of communication, and despite the emphasis on the teaching of culture in the standards, Renate A. Schulz points out that there are problems in implementing the standards with respect to culture, not the least of which are the lack of adequate teacher preparation in the area of culture and the lack of a definition of *culture* common to all foreign language professionals (2007, 10–12). Then, too, there are basic problems of curricular selection when the instructor is faced with the challenge of highlighting diversity among the speakers of a given language.

Thus, the goal of teaching language in context becomes problematic. In "knowing how, when, and why to say what to whom" (American Council on the Teaching of Foreign Languages n.d.) the "what" (vocabulary) and the "how" (grammar) may be somewhat determined by the "when" (conditions) and the "why" (purpose), themselves dependent on the "whom" (audience). For instance, knowing how to give a compliment entails knowing when and why such a speech act would be appropriate. That compliment may take on a very different form if the recipient is a businesswoman in Panama City versus an elderly farmer in rural Spain.

FROM THE "MELTING POT" TO THE "SALAD BOWL"

Students are typically unaware that they are going to study a range of cultures bound by common language. To many, French is spoken only in France, German in Germany, and Spanish in Mexico, and there are no regional variations. Indeed, classroom discussions frequently reveal the extent to which they believe that all young people are fundamentally like themselves with the same values, priorities, and behaviors. To them, there is no real other. However, there may be pseudo-others, superficially different, but essentially not unlike the norm. In Disneyland's famous ride, the animatronic figures differ in physical characteristics, setting, garb, and language, but even as the spectator glides through distinctly themed rooms, the similarity among the childlike inhabitants cannot be missed.

The foreign language teacher in a "melting pot" setting has ostensibly been handed a gift. First, it is easy and emotionally gratifying to chip away at the students' illusions of universal sameness. "Us-them" comparisons are more easily drawn when a homogenous group compares and contrasts itself with a monolithic other. Second, culturally shared understandings facilitate teaching language through context.

There are also obvious pitfalls to teaching in the "melting pot." "Us-them" comparisons rely heavily on generalizations and stereotypes. Without readily apparent cultural variety in the classroom to nuance learners' perceptions of who they are as a group, they are more likely to accept blanket statements unquestioningly. It would be too easy for the teacher to replace a "we are all alike" mentality with an "us versus them" way of seeing the world, an artificial dichotomy that could lead to the development of a sense of cultural superiority or inferiority.

Since the terrorist attacks of September 11, 2001, and the subsequent harassment of American Muslims, "us versus them" comparisons must particularly be avoided in classrooms. Moreover, taking advantage of the supposed homogeneity of a class in order to create context-based lessons entails the troublesome inevitability that there might actually be diversity present among the students that goes unnoticed, suppressed by a student who is eager to conform to the mainstream or overlooked by the teacher who becomes so blinded by sameness that she or he fails to notice difference.

I teach at Georgia Gwinnett College (GGC), located in Gwinnett County, which is ethnically and linguistically diverse. The U.S. Census Bureau estimated that, in 2006–2010, 25.5 percent of Gwinnett County residents were foreign born (compared with 9.6 percent in the state of Georgia) and that 32.2 percent of residents aged five or older speak a language other than English at home (compared with 12.7 percent statewide; U.S. Census Bureau n.d.). Gwinnett County is "salad bowl" America rather than "melting pot" America.

A melting pot dissolves metals together until a new alloy forms, its components indistinguishable. In the salad bowl, individual components remain identifiable and distinct, although the longer an item sits in a salad, the more it takes on the flavor of the other ingredients and influences the whole with its own flavor.

GGC students are a mix of white and black southerners, transplants from other regions of the United States; recent immigrants, including refugees; generation 1.5 students who spent most, if not all, of their formative years in the United States; and international students. While the "melting pot" and "salad bowl" metaphors have been solely used to name processes of assimilation regarding race and national origin, the theories of intersectionality argue that an individual's perspective, sense of self, and access to advantage is determined by a confluence of demographic factors.

Pedagogies inspired by the literature on intersectionality caution against using prompts that are too culturally specific when assessing students. For example, in classes I have taught, testing materials include such questions in French as "What genre of film do you associate with John Wayne?" (*un western*, or "a western") and "What was the profession of Mark Twain?" (*un écrivain*, or "a writer"), but some immigrant students have not heard of these men.

During one oral exam, a student from Central Africa was asked to describe a picture of a woman in a hospital bed holding a newborn and flanked by two women in medical uniforms. The picture should have elicited vocabulary like *l'hôpital* (the hospital), *le médecin* (the doctor), or *l'infirmière* (the nurse), but instead the student said that these women were the sisters of the new mother. This student may not have been familiar with the trappings of an American hospital, instead activating different cultural assumptions about who would be present at a birth.

An oral exam for a third-semester course required students to view a brief commercial and narrate what they saw in French. I had to suspend the use of one commercial, because it was culturally problematic. In a public service announcement warning of the dangers of anorexia, one sees a slightly overweight girl scrutinizing her body in a mirror, but then the camera pulls back to reveal that she is actually dangerously emaciated. Only her reflection (her imagined self) is overweight. Eating disorders and idealized thin body types are phenomena associated with the developed world. Therefore, several students misunderstood the imagery. One student (originally from a "developing" country) struggled so much to relate what he saw that it finally occurred to me to ask him in English if he knew what anorexia was. He did not. The problem lay not in his French but in his lack of familiarity with a disorder that is undoubtedly less prevalent and less publicized in the "developing" world. Even when students told me that they knew what anorexia was, it did not mean they understood the commercial as a Westerner might. For example, one student thought that the video showed two sisters, one of whom suffered from an eating disorder. Another student understood that the anorexic girl was looking in the mirror but interpreted the "overweight" girl in the reflection as an idealized, healthy self rather than as an irrational and repugnant self-image. When an exam question is so fraught with the possibility of misunderstanding, it is unusable. Assessments in foreign language courses should include contextualized tasks; however, it may be useful to find prompts that are as culturally neutral as possible.

IMPLICATIONS ACROSS THE CURRICULUM

While this chapter focuses on the problem of teaching culture-bound foreign languages to culturally diverse classes, it does raise issues that are pertinent to other academic subjects and classroom practice in general. Even as students are trained to question assumptions, gather data, experiment, build arguments, and express themselves according to the standards of a discipline, even as they are taught that opinions are not equally valid, courses must be designed to draw students into open discourse in such a way that they are less likely to suppress their differences. To that end, there are three guiding principles and corresponding objectives:

1. *Respect*: Students will show respect not only for the practices and products they observe in the target culture(s) (that is, the culture[s] under examination) but also for those cultural practices and products they observe among themselves.
2. *Curiosity*: Students will demonstrate curiosity about products, practices, and paradoxes of the target culture; examine and analyze their own practices; seek cultural variances in their own communities; and wonder about the reasons, origins, and destinies of cultural practices and products.
3. *Critical Thinking*: Students will construct guidelines for intercultural interactions based on their observations of the target culture, distinguish general cultural trends from individual and personal behavior, and identify real and potential positive and negative outcomes of various practices in the target culture and in their own.

Respect

Respect is the first goal because it is unquestionably the most crucial for creating a sense of inclusion in the classroom. Inclusion should not entail students being put "on display" or treated as if they must represent a group. Speaking as a black, it is wearying to frequently have to speak as a black.

However, a person's experience is conditioned by her or his belonging to that group, and it would be disrespectful not to recognize this fact.

Then again, the group in question may not be the one with which a person (myself) identifies most strongly. She may be more comfortable speaking as a woman or as a southerner or as an academic than as a black. Perhaps she feels that those identities have had a greater impact on shaping her perspectives or are more salient in a specific context. On the other hand, if she chooses to speak as a black, then she should not be accused of "playing the race card." It is as disrespectful to deny her the right to act as representative of her group as it is to expect her to perform that function, if she is unwilling to do it.

I want all my students to feel what Bernardo M. Ferdman describes as the experience of inclusion: "When an individual experiences inclusion, she or he feels fully present and involved, believes that others recognize and appreciate his or her contributions, and feels both safe and open about his or her social identities" (Ferdman 2010, 2). However, there is a risk that one student may disdain the social identity of another or dismiss another's right to represent a given group. Still, perhaps the greatest lapse takes place when the instructor as the authority figure calls on a student to represent a social group. It happens quite innocently and usually involves a young person of francophone descent or origin in French classes. "You're French. Tell us, what was school like when you were little?" "Your family is from Senegal. Tell us, what languages do members of your family speak?"

It is very tempting to treat students as supplements to the textbook when they have relevant lived experience that their instructor lacks. Whether the instructor's questions are personal or designed to elicit generalizations, they may be unwelcome by the student who is suddenly put in the position of cultural ambassador. This issue is particularly acute when the student does not feel "both safe and open about his or her social identities." Paradoxically, while an environment of respect is indispensable for enabling the experience of inclusion, a respectful instructor must accept that perfect inclusion may not be possible. For historical reasons, individual learners in a diverse class—a lesbian, a Latino, a self-proclaimed "redneck"—will feel that certain facets of who they are will be disparaged, trivialized, or attacked if brought into the open.

Derek R. Avery and Kecia M. Thomas point out that students from the dominant group may keep silent when the issue of diversity arises in order to avoid being perceived as politically incorrect, whereas members of a disadvantaged group may remain mum to keep from drawing attention to themselves or to avoid the negative consequences of talking about differences experienced in previous classes (2004, 387). Some students may not wish to share their perspectives as a member of a socially disadvantaged group, and indeed secrecy may be an integral aspect of how members of one group interact with the larger world. For example, immigrant and refugee students who were contending with personal or communal trauma are sometimes unwilling to share their experiences in class (Fong 2004, 51). College is a time of growth and transition, and a student's sense of how she or he fits into social categories may be very much in flux. Some students may not feel that they can participate fully because they belong to groups that have traditionally been intolerant to or advantaged vis-à-vis others. For example, an ultra-conservative student knows that his or her homophobic beliefs and attitudes about gender must be abandoned or suppressed in order to interact with LGBTQ or feminist classmates. It is worth remembering that religious identity and cultural value systems are not always a matter of personal choice. Instructors must walk the line of demonstrating respect to all students while communicating clearly that insensitive language and intolerant attitudes—which may be central to a person's sense of identity—are unwelcome and unhelpful.

Curiosity

Respect is somewhat related to the second guiding principle: curiosity. On more than one occasion, students have expressed to the instructor their reticence to study a foreign language ("Everyone speaks English anyway!") or even to take a history class other than U.S. history ("I'm an American. I need to study my own history."). In order to develop lifelong learners who *want* to explore that which is foreign in their own communities and the world at large, courses must cultivate curiosity. In higher education, curiosity may be seen as a "threat" to the curriculum. Professors feel that they must "cover" an enormous amount of material in a short time and may communicate to their students that tangential questions rob the class of the time needed to meet the course objectives.

Curious students sometimes behave as if they are entitled to answers, no matter how uncomfortable the subject, simply because they want to know, even if it means forcing a classmate into assuming the role of spokesperson for a group. Then there are the students whose questions are purely rhetorical because they have already made up their minds on the topic at hand. Such students are not curious about the perspectives of others, although they may be curious about the reactions they will elicit in others.

So here is the conundrum: How can educators encourage curiosity while protecting a tight schedule and a respectful classroom culture? David Wong suggests giving students a bit more space and time to explore their curiosities but encouraging them to become curious about a range of topics, so that they do not sacrifice learning in a variety of areas to a singular obsession (2012, 64–65). Susan Engel advocates creating activities that require students to "figure out what they want to know and then seek answers," taking care to guide them in evaluating sources and testing hypotheses (2013, 40).

Malcolm S. Knowles, Elwood F. Holton III, and Richard A. Swanson point out that, in the pedagogical model of instruction, there is a limiting assumption about what the learner needs to know: "Learners only need to know that they must learn what the teacher teaches if they want to pass and get promoted; they do not need to know how what they learn will apply to their lives" (1998, 62). Internal motivators, such as curiosity, are irrelevant, as is the experience of the learner, and students "see learning as acquiring subject-matter content" (Knowles, Holton, and Swanson 1998, 63), the scope and sequence of which are determined by the teacher.

In contrast, the andragogical model assumes that learners "need to know why they need to learn something before they undertake to learn it" (Knowles, Holton, and Swanson 1998, 64); that their motivation to learn is chiefly internal; that they have a life-centered—rather than subject-centered—orientation to learning; and that they have an ever-widening range of experiences and learn most effectively when they can draw on these experiences (Knowles, Holton, and Swanson 1998, 68).

Creating time and space to allow students to demonstrate curiosity about their own practices and communities means structuring the course with an andragogical approach from the outset. Ferdman recognizes that a teacher cannot impart inclusion to students without modeling it, which means ceding some control: "Teaching inclusion requires addressing issues in the moment, as they arise, in the context of an overall plan. It requires being aware of and capitalizing on here-and-now dynamics and possibilities, as well as wholeheartedly engaging with students and treating them as full learning partners" (2010, 3).

Critical Thinking

Of course, even adult students do not necessarily wish to be "full learning partners," and many simply prefer the pedagogical model they have always known, a model that allows them to check their curiosity and experience at the classroom door. Yet, students must be fully present and engaged in order to achieve the third goal for contextualized learning in an inclusive class: critical thinking.

In a diverse classroom, there is a range in intellectual development, especially at an institution with an open-access mission. Students who believe in a single and uncomplicated "correct" answer may be the victims of internalized hegemonic understandings, whether they themselves benefit from them or are oppressed by them. That is, a student from a dominant group may assume that the "right answer" is aligned with her or his own experiences or worldview, while a student from a disadvantaged group may feel that she or he can never know the right answer without being informed by an authoritative source. Learners from disadvantaged groups may start to believe that there is a single "correct" answer for academic purposes (an answer that students must learn in order to get a good grade) but that there is also a "real" correct answer that conforms to her or his understanding of the world, an answer that has no place in the academy.

An instructor can model the importance of individual experiences in class discussions by pointing out when her own questions, perceptions, and analyses are informed by her experiences as a woman, a black, a southerner, an academic, a mother, a middle-class person, an Anglophone, a U.S. citizen, a heterosexual, and so forth. Such strategies help the students to understand that the accrual of reliable knowledge is neither a neutral nor a purely personal enterprise. An appreciation of this fact can nuance students' understandings of world events and customs.

CONCLUSION

Teaching content through context serves students well, particularly in foreign language courses, wherein communicative acts must be situated within cultural frameworks. On the other hand, there are risks of homogenizing the target culture into a convenient stereotype, of treating the class as culturally monolithic (a melting pot) rather than recognizing the diversity present (a salad bowl and a site of intersecting categories), or of assuming that a context presented to the group will be uniformly understood by the individual learners. While these points are especially salient in the field of foreign languages, any educator who teaches global topics to a culturally diverse group should work toward the goal of inclusion, promoting three interrelated guiding principles: respect, curiosity, and critical thinking.

In diverse classrooms, frequent guided collaborations among students should allow them to practice openness, vulnerability, and risk-taking in cross-cultural communication but also to exercise mutual respect and curiosity and, on good days, critical thinking. An andragogical approach that honors the experience-centered, purpose-driven orientation of learners dictates that students must develop sensitivity to the instructional use of context.

Chapter Six

Beyond the Accent

Intersectionality in a Foreign-Trained Instructor Classroom

Josephine J. Dawuni

Students in Western educational institutions who are confronted with the question "What is the biggest challenge you face in a class taught by a foreign-trained professor?" are likely to respond, "She has an accent. I do not understand her." This study is set in the context of the American college experience, where a foreign accent has become an essentialized problem, often blurring the many other challenges that both students and foreign-trained instructors (FTIs, born abroad and trained abroad, at least in their undergraduate education) face in the classroom.

Studies on intercultural classroom communications show that the construction of identity categories often begins with how a person sounds and whether the intonation is different from the hearer's (Fleisher, Masinori, and Weinberg 2002; Kavas and Kavas 2008; Rao 1995). Culture and language are closely intertwined. Thus, in teaching environments, cultural differences in teaching and learning may be misunderstood as a language problem (Kavas and Kavas 2008).

Aysel Kavas and Alican Kavas (2008) undertook a study involving forty-five faculty who identified themselves as foreign born, representing twenty-four countries, and ninety-one students who identified themselves as native born or American. The results indicated that 42.9 percent of the respondents felt the "pronunciation and accent" of the instructor was very important to their learning.

Studies by Belton Fleisher, Hashimoto Masinori, and Bruce A. Weinberg based on interviews of foreign-born teaching assistants demonstrated otherwise. Their studies showed that classes taught by foreign-trained instructors had high levels of student performance and low dropout rates. Yet, when it came to evaluating the teaching effectiveness of these instructors, the student opinions were low, not necessarily because of the language gap, but rather due to other cultural gaps, such as interpersonal skills and cultural differences (Fleisher, Masinori, and Weinberg 2002).

However, other studies have concluded that the "accent" of FTIs can be a real problem for some students (Lippi-Green 1997; Rao 1995; and many others). How can an instructor achieve the goal of getting students to understand her or his "foreignness" (aspects of an individual's identity, such as race, ethnicity, and cultural and linguistic attributes, which make her or him distinct from the local long-term residents) in the classroom and embrace it as part of the learning experience, not an obstacle?

This chapter contributes to the growing literature on intersectionality by arguing that, in navigating a classroom, FTIs must move beyond the accent and look at the underlying factors, such as culture, gender, and power. To advance this argument, this chapter explores the following questions: First, which intersecting identities are created by culture, gender, and power in a college classroom? Second, what are the effects of these identities on the teaching and learning environment? Third, how can instructors and students make good use of these identities to make the classroom environment emancipatory?

THEORETICAL FRAMEWORK

The concept of intersectionality, though relatively new, remains a contested method of scientific inquiry. First expounded by Crenshaw (1989; 1991), it is a theoretical approach that examines how different identities intersect to create power and subordination in society. Though the initial focus was on women, especially black women as a minority group, the concept has been broadened to examine multiple identities in society, such as those of race (Abes, Jones, and McEwen 2007), sexual orientation (Weber 1998), and the use of language (Sharplin 2009).

FTIs often find themselves placed at the intersection of multiple identities, such as race, gender, ethnicity, and national origin—each of these belonging to categories that can be mutually reinforcing. It is often the case that these categories also expose foreign teachers to oppressive and sometimes hostile attitudes from students and colleagues who resist "foreignness," irrespective of inherent advantages that come with that category. Without dwelling too much on the negative, it is worth pointing out that the category of "foreignness" also comes with certain advantages, which are discussed in detail later in this chapter. Intersectionality allows a deeper investigation into how multiple identities (culture, gender, and power) and social contexts within the classroom may provide the answers to underlying questions of difference faced by college students and professors.

CULTURE

The first question related to culture that most professors face is "Where do you come from?" For an instructor who gets a new group of students every semester, it feels as if the proverbial "culture shock" never ends, as one is continually seeking new ways to explore and overcome this glaring challenge of one's "otherness." The cultural challenges are not limited to one's "foreignness" alone but may include issues related to pedagogy, classroom management, the use of language, or the accent factor (Sharplin 2009).

Culture can be conceptualized in terms of *language* as a cultural identity. An accent is part of this identity. Richards, Platt, and Platt define *accent* as a "particular way of speaking which tells the listener something about the speaker's background" (1992, 1). However, language becomes a problem when some students blame their weak performances in class on the fact that the instructor had an "accent." Nonetheless, this "language barrier" can lead to enrichment as well. Some students may see it as a challenge that must be overcome, causing them to listen more attentively in class, talk to the professor after class, and seek other ways to learn outside the classroom. Thus, the challenge of the language barrier consequently helps to improve the overall performance of the students in class, while enriching their global knowledge.

The language barrier can also lead to *intercultural communication apprehension*, which may arise in students from the very first day of class (Neuliep and McCroskey 1997). The apprehension some students face could lead to a reduction in student comfort in the class and consequently to the student's receptivity (or lack thereof) of the content of instruction, no matter how good a teacher the instructor may be.

In a study conducted by Kavas and Kavas (2008), of a sample of ninety-one students, 36.3 percent indicated that the instructor's use of humor was an important part of the learning process. This can be a slippery ground to stand on because what constitutes humor in one culture may not necessarily be humorous in another. Therefore, one must be careful with the use of humor in cross-cultural environments, as it could become a source of misunderstanding.

Studies examining student receptivity to perceived professional credentials of their teachers reveal that students in American classrooms tend to view favorably and are often more receptive to the teachers of European origin when compared with black teachers (Bower 2002; Vargas 2002). Perceptions of cultural differences do play an important role in the perceived effectiveness of foreign-trained teachers. This is often evidenced in class-room evaluations where FTIs tend to score low on questions that seek to establish their effectiveness in the delivery of class content (McCroskey 2002).

GENDER

Gender as an identity construct manifests along different dimensions in high-er education with multiple implications, which can be both empowering and subordinating (Dill 2002; Valentine 2007; Weber 1998). The challenges posed by gender as an identity construct can be especially disempowering if one's gender is further located within the identity of a minority race or ethnicity. In the United States, women of color tend to face disproportionate-ly higher subordination from students, faculty, and wider educational institu-tional structures (Allison 2008; Harris 2007; Patitu and Hinton 2003; and many others). The challenges that women face are translated into annual evaluations, often showing lower mean scores for minority female faculty as compared with their white female counterparts. In one study that examined student evaluation of instructor effectiveness, the findings demonstrate that non-Caucasian female faculty had average lower scores when compared with their Caucasian female counterparts (B. Smith and Johnson-Bailey 2011).

Gender remains an important component of social identity that cuts across different cultures, yet the challenges posed by being a woman and a racial minority produces multiple hierarchies that must be addressed in the classroom. The perceived notions of a woman as "weak" may be interpreted as grounds by some students to reproduce societal norms of gender insubor-dination in the classroom (by challenging the authority of teachers who are women).

POWER

Power differentials in the classroom can create and reinforce inequality and subordination, which is at the very heart of intersectionality. Depending on how the teachers use their power relative to the students' perception of their teachers' power can lead to either an empowering or disempowering of stu-dents or instructors. The role of power as an identity and its intersection with other social constructs can create multiple layers of identity existing side by side as oppression or privilege (Dill, McLaughlin, and Nieves 2007).

The growing body of literature on tolerance education shows that minor-ity teachers, identified either by race, ethnicity, or gender, tend to be the disproportionate recipients of power challenges in the classroom (Patton and Catching 2009). Students often perceive and therefore rate the role of FTIs' teaching effectiveness, student engagement, and ability to answer questions as inadequate (Bower 2002). International teachers may be perceived in the United States as having to learn from "us" (that is, the Americans) and not to teach "us," mirroring the power dynamic that can find its way into the FTIs' classrooms (Mestenhauser 1983).

Similarly, minority teachers (blacks, Latinas, Latinos, and FTIs) experience constant scrutiny by some students who perceive their own "majority" status as linked to power and privilege. The existence of such perceived power differences in the classroom may result in viewing the teacher as ineffective and less knowledgeable and therefore subject to student attacks and criticisms (Thomas and Hollenshead 2001; Turner 2002). The effect of such power dynamics can lead to some explosive exchanges in the classroom.

IDENTITIES AND EXPERIENCES

The intercultural classroom is not situated above identities within society at large. In fact, the classroom in many ways mirrors different and sometimes conflicting societal identities. In classroom experiences I have encountered, different student and instructor identities have in most cases produced positive outcomes, where the instructor's "otherness" has been a useful tool. This is especially so in teaching and introducing subjects that are foreign, intriguing, and engaging to the students who may have never had such experiences in the past or have not been exposed to such knowledge.

Changes must take place not only in the classroom but also, even more importantly, at the institutional level. The growing literature on tolerance education provides some insights on how institutions can transform their climates to be more accommodating of FTIs. There are many challenges and hurdles to be overcome by foreign FTIs, but it would be helpful if instructors themselves focus on the advantages that they bring to the institutions and the classrooms rather than dwell on the negative challenges (Gahungu 2011).

RECOMMENDATIONS FOR INTEGRATION

How can instructors and students make good use of intersecting identities to make the classroom environment emancipatory? Instructors are given a special mandate to teach their students to the best of their abilities and to make the classrooms welcoming learning environments. While occasional challenges and issues may arise, it is still the duty of instructors to ensure that class time and candor are used to achieve the ultimate goals of teaching and learning. For this reason, the imagery of the ship on the high seas may be relevant here as a uniting metaphor, capable of transcending different interests. Here, the instructor is the captain of the ship, and she (or he) controls the direction of the vessel. The students are the crew and passengers, who must cooperate with the authority and respect the instruction of the captain to make for an easy journey and safe arrival at their destination. Following this metaphor, a successful classroom experience requires the cooperation of both the instructor and the students.

The following recommendations may be helpful in maximizing learning outcomes. First, the instructor must be in charge of the classroom. Taking charge does not necessarily mean using the instructor's perceived power to create vertical hierarchies in the class but rather taking charge to allow each student a voice in the classroom. Allowing students to have a voice may include encouraging student participation in classroom discussions, inviting and encouraging discussion on controversial issues, and gently redirecting students to pertinent and relevant discussion without shutting them down.

Second, it is essential for the instructor to identify and acknowledge her or his personal social identities and use those identities as an empowering and vital tool for teaching. As the captain of the class (the ship), it is the instructor's duty to steer the ship the way she or he thinks is best for promoting learning and active student engagement in class. However, this should be done while keeping in mind that a successful learning environment benefits both the instructor and students.

Third, instructors should be cognizant of student identities and seek ways, as much as possible, to conduct the teaching in a way that emphasizes positive identities while deemphasizing negative ones. Using an inclusionary perspective, the instructor can emphasize to students the importance of being heard, thus removing the element of subordination and power dominance, where the instructor does all the talking and the students are reduced to passive listeners. In addition, the instructor should encourage students to share their local and global experiences as a way of getting all voices to be heard in the classroom.

Close attention needs to be paid to drawing in foreign students, who often tend to be quiet participants in the classroom because of such issues as their accents. For instance, the use of inclusive language when teaching about American politics, with such words as *we* and *us*, can demonstrate to the students that the issues discussed in a political science class to a large extent affects almost everyone in the class, though to varying degrees. This strategy tends to reduce (though not totally prevent) the notion of the "us versus them" mentality that is often a dividing wall between teaching and student receptivity to certain realities.

Fourth, instructors should seek ways to develop effective interpersonal communication skills to engage their students. In developing approaches to get students to understand the instructor and engage with her or him, it is important for instructors to remind themselves that they are in the classroom because of the students. Hence, the onus lies heavily on the instructor to make students feel at ease in understanding and being receptive to the material being taught. For example, when the instructor uses a word that students may not understand, she or he can try repeating the word and writing it on the board.

Fifth, attempts should be made to develop strategies aimed at minimizing the gap between cultures. Often I infuse my teaching with tales from personal experiences, travels, and encounters with other people around the world, highlighting cultural differences and commonalities. Instructors should be aware of cultural differences but not consumed by them. Rather, they should accept their foreignness as a valuable resource and use it to help their students to become interculturally competent and globally aware.

Sixth, FTIs can make the teaching and learning experience more enjoyable for both parties by using practical examples within the local context that are familiar to the students (J. Smith, Meyers, and Burkhalter 1992). In addition, instructors can refine their teaching methods by paying closer attention to how they handle questions and the clarity of their responses to questions posed by students.

CONCLUSION

This chapter demonstrates the complex ways in which multilayered identities, such as culture, gender, and power, may combine to create a transformative classroom. How can instructors create an emancipatory classroom that allows for the interplay of multiple identities? How can instructors give voice to students who feel their culture is "under attack" by a foreign professor?

In answering these questions, it is important to stress that students by no means share one culture. The existence of multilayered and intersecting cultures makes it a difficult task for an instructor to navigate the intersecting identity contours. How successful one is at dealing with these different identities is dependent on different factors, some of which are presented in this chapter. Feminist pedagogy may be instructive here, as it reminds the instructor to aim for making the classroom experience an interactive one, one that allows both students and the teacher to be subjects and not objects of the learning process (Shrewsbury 1993).

The arguments advanced in this chapter strongly suggest that an interactive classroom experience is possible when multiple layers of identities in the classroom are identified. This allows the instructor to peel away at each layer as a way of getting to the core of what is being taught and how it is being taught. Instructors can create an engaging classroom that moves beyond social identities and barriers. They should seek a common ground for creating a learning experience that is both engaging and liberating. Education should be a process where students get to engage in critical thinking, to question identities, and to seek solutions to oppression (hooks 1994).

Chapter Seven

Lie to Me

Learning about Manipulation on Social Media through Operation Design

Ignas Kalpokas

The chapter explores my practices in teaching a module on information security, influence operations, and weaponization of social media in political science classes. As part of the module, the students are asked to prepare a plan for a fictitious social media psychological influence operation. The operation plan includes the intended target, the messages to be promoted, the aims to be achieved, a step-by-step description of the actions to be taken, and a list of criteria to evaluate the outcomes. The final operation design is presented in class.

Far from being a trivial addition to teaching and assessment, this strategy has clear ethical and educational benefits, particularly in a diverse environment. The ethical benefit pertains to one's own position as a lecturer and whether an objective, nonmanipulated stance, cleansed of all influence operations, is possible or desirable. Hence, the strategy I have adopted is to present students with the basic techniques used to carry out influence operations, subsequently allowing them to conduct their own research. Diversity of opinions is fostered by allowing the students to speak for themselves and for the views they hold.

In terms of educational benefits, students are taught to be critical consumers of information without privileging a particular worldview. Students are taught how manipulation on social media works, hopefully making them better equipped to recognize influence operations. Also, discussions following presentations make students more aware of the variety of standpoints and experiences, thus further fostering the experience of the multiple ways in which our reality is constructed.

AN IMPORTANT BUT INHERENTLY PROBLEMATIC SUBJECT

Strategic communication, influence campaigns, or psychological operations (often abbreviated as "psyops") employing social media are crucial aspects of today's conflicts (also of pre- and postconflict situations) and of latent threats, such as terrorist recruitment (e.g., Collings and Rohozinski 2009; Kalpokas 2016; Lange-Ionatamishvili and Svetoka 2015; NATO STRAT-COM 2015a; NATO STRATCOM 2015b; NATO STRATCOM 2015c). Hence, it is extremely important to introduce students, especially in communications or politics-related programs, to the complexities of weaponized information.

In fact, social media are an ideal environment in which to "mobilize, intimidate or terrorize a targeted population" and cause physical effects without physical presence (Yannakogeorgos 2014, 57). Broadly, then, *psyops* can be defined as sustained and targeted employment of particular narratives, directed at the civilian population or the military (or both), intended to change the target group's perception of themselves and of a larger body (e.g., their state). Such operations blur the distinction between war and peace and have added new and increased avenues for propaganda and manipulation.

Social media influence campaigns have created a new phenomenon—"sofa warriors." These are individuals who often do not have a political agenda and are unconscious of their role but still help further a psyop by partaking in online groups and sharing specific information. Hence, education is particularly important. It is only by improving critical thinking and media literacy skills that immunity to such influence operations can be strengthened.

However, precisely the sheer ubiquity and imperceptiveness of such operations raise questions regarding one's supposedly objective and privileged status as a lecturer. "Sofa warriors" disseminate psyop content in much the same way as conventional malware is propagated. They can be employed for dissemination of the message (enlarging the network); low-level background activity (sustaining the information environment); or orchestrated large-scale operations in which large amounts of psyop messages are disseminated together with political, military, or other moves.

Consequently, one might reasonably expect disagreements over what students accept to be legitimate truth claims, and the more this is true, the more diverse the class is. After all, it is a well-known truism that one man's terrorist is another man's freedom fighter. And in terms of teaching psyops, that logic is especially evident. As a result, there is a need for an approach that takes students' views regardless of their and the lecturer's particular standpoints. A task requiring construction of fictional influence campaigns instead of an in-class analysis of real ones is precisely such a strategy.

The course plan usually is as follows: First, preconditions of social media influence operations are presented. These include globalization, Web 2.0, the rise of social media, and the social and political changes associated with the "new" media. Then, the students are introduced to the general principles of psyops, their history, and possible applications. Finally, the specific techniques and methods of their application are looked at but with an effort to only use fictitious examples whenever possible. All of this is intended to equip students with the knowledge to then develop their own fictional campaigns.

NOW DO IT YOURSELF: LIE TO ME

As already noted, students are asked to present a fictional influence campaign in class (followed by an essay that further elaborates the main points). They are free to choose both the target and the perpetrator of the psyop but are advised against using real-life actors, especially as perpetrators. Regardless of the parties involved, students are asked to explain why this particular context and actors have been selected and why an analysis of such a psyop is timely and relevant.

This requirement is specifically aimed to make students think about the current political and economic context and the most likely or dangerous information conflicts at that particular time. Then, students are expected to clearly state the goals of their influence campaigns and present the means to achieve them. The goals must clearly relate to the actors and the situations chosen. Likewise, the means must specifically contribute to the stated goals, as opposed to being just random ideas. The means themselves involve specific techniques of influence as well as methods of applying these techniques. Again, students are expected to be able to embed a sense of purpose into their selection of means and to be able to recognize such means when they are applied in real-life situations.

Finally, the third part of the presentation is dedicated to the expected outcomes and ways of measuring the success of the influence operation. Emphasis here is, again, on context and an understanding of what such an attack is likely or would need to achieve under given circumstances. On the one hand, that means adding some moderation into the assessment of psyops (they cannot achieve everything and under all circumstances and have to be directed with precision), but on the other hand, this reflection also encourages students to think about the variety of situation-specific aims that influence campaigns can be expected to achieve.

Such presentations can only work for relatively small groups of students (I have only practiced them with groups of up to twenty students). It would, perhaps, be too difficult to apply the method to larger classes. Presenting in groups might be an option.

THE BENEFITS OF CREATING A PSYOP

Tasking students with researching and developing their own campaigns can be seen as beneficial in itself. Student research enhances independent critical thinking (Buckley 2011; Kinkead 2003), expands their experience and horizons (Löfström 2011), and positively affects education in general (Russell, Hancock, and McCullough 2007). Also, inquiry-based teaching is particularly handy when competing interpretations of events are present, as it is more likely to defuse any potential conflicts than narrative-based teaching (McCully 2012). The latter aspect is of particular importance to teaching psyops.

Allowing students to present their own fictional cases does not require the presence of a shared frame of reference. In fact, because students are presenting *fictional* influence campaigns, most disagreements about the real world are rendered irrelevant. Rather than oppressively asserting a particular position, such presentations foster diversity by allowing every student not only to have an opinion but also to meaningfully contribute to the learning process.

Also, indirectly, the presentations help to teach students to be more critical consumers of information without privileging a single worldview and simultaneously stigmatizing some members of the group by branding what they believe is wrong. Such stigmatization is more likely to reduce a student's aptitude to contribute and, even more significantly, diminish the receptiveness to information while simultaneously giving the students impetus to further defensively entrench themselves in their worldviews.

In many ways, the problem in question is very similar to the debate surrounding ideology. Indeed, instead of the traditional way of treating ideological thinking as "false consciousness," today the trend is toward refutation of the temptation to correct or to pass judgment (Freeden 2016). Ideologies are now usually treated as simply social forms of cognition that are shared within specific groups (van Dijk 2013). A similar approach is recommended when teaching psyops.

The issue here is not even about truly or wrongly representing certain campaigns as psyops. The problem is about interpreting them, which not only presupposes that the interpreter's point of view is uninfluenced but also unavoidably imbues any content to be discussed by the particularities of the interpreter's person. On the one hand, this "contamination" is an unavoidable part of any representation (Petrescu 2015). On the other hand, influence operations are a delicate enough subject for even differences in nuance to have significant effect as to the students' perceptions of their peers and of the class as such.

It is almost a truism that "ideologies . . . are typically attributed to Others. . . . *We* have the truth, *They* have ideologies" (van Dijk 2013, 175). The same applies to psyops: *We* possess an uninfluenced worldview, while *they* are being manipulated. And yet, this is a mental shortcut. In fact, rejecting the importance of influence on one's own thinking means shutting away a crucial avenue of analysis and unduly diminishing the self-awareness of everyone involved.

The latter point signals yet another benefit of constructing fictional influence campaigns. It has already been asserted that students' critical thinking skills are enhanced by independently adopting the techniques commonly used in psyops and that, as a result, students can be expected to recognize the same techniques directed toward them. In addition, both the method and the diversity of perspectives (in conjunction with the knowledge of techniques) are expected to also foster self-reflection: the students would be enabled to sift through not only external messages but also ideas that are already held for certain.

There is also a further argument: In an educational environment, the normative value of worldviews promoted through psyops does not depend on facts. Even if there was a hypothetically ideal situation in which two competing narratives were being promoted in an attempt to affect a population's thinking and behavior on a certain issue and one of them could be undeniably proven as based purely on fact and the other purely on fiction, they would both be categorized as influence campaigns. Indeed, it is the technique—the form—and not the content that should be the object of analysis. Just like other controversial terms, such as *ideology*, *influence operation* is not a pejorative description but merely an analytical category. Hence, an external criterion of truthfulness for deciding between different psyops is invalidated. Indeed, it is paramount that, in an educational environment, parity between different subject positions is maintained (Norman 2012), and this principle is of particular relevance when teaching psyops.

A crucial difference must be stressed here: one between a primarily educational agenda and one primarily concerned with national (or business) security. Contrary to the educational approach, the security one must stress the primacy of some influence operations and some worldviews over others. That is because somebody concerned with security is an open and legitimate proponent of a particular worldview, while from an academic standpoint, all influence campaigns are equal.

Of course, teaching has to be based on some values and promote some ideas that form the core of societies (e.g., that misogyny or racism is inherently wrong). However, beyond that, it is debated whether teaching should have emancipatory goals (for such a teleological approach, see Carmigian

2013); instead, students should be allowed to make up their own minds based on the information available. It is of no help for students' critical thinking skills if following a perpetrator of an influence campaign is replaced with following the lecturer as yet another influencer.

A CAUTIONARY NOTE ON ETHICS AND SECURITY

Student research and projects, such as modeling of psyops in particular, have their own ethical challenges. The material accessed and used, as well as the propositions made, can easily prove to be objectionable from the standpoint of research ethics. As a result, some authors (notably, Doyle and Buckley 2014; P. Smith and Rust 2011) go as far as to suggest that all student research, including at the undergraduate level, should get clearance from an institutional research ethics committee just like any other kind of research. I do not necessarily subscribe to the bureaucratization of the research-teaching nexus. However, it is true that some ethical guidance as to the responsibilities pertaining to a task that requires creation of a strategy for manipulating the human mind is necessary. Also, some protections of having obtained an ethics clearance would also be welcome, as some cases in the British academia attest.

Perhaps the best-known case was that of a University of Nottingham student who, along with his acquaintance (an employee at the same university), was arrested and interrogated on terrorism charges after having downloaded an al-Qaeda training manual as part of research for his master's thesis (Curtis and Hodgson 2008). Despite the manual in question being a widely used research resource, freely available on a U.S. government website, the university not only failed to support the student but also, on the contrary, appeared to be acting on the presumption of guilt (Gallagher 2011; Gill 2011). More recently, another student was put under investigation for reading a book on terrorism studies at Staffordshire University's library, again as part of his research (Sherriff 2015).

Certainly, terrorism is an exceptionally sensitive subject in Western societies. Also, one might stipulate that the aforementioned cases are just a few instances of institutions overreacting or that, even in the West, such sensitivity is rather country-specific. These are reasonable objections. However, it must still be stressed that this particular exercise requires special oversight. First, this is because students may delve into some dubious material for inspiration; second, the content itself could easily arouse suspicion (e.g., a student creating a pro-Islamist psyop). As a result, students cannot be left on their own.

It is of paramount importance that, even if full research ethics clearance is not deemed necessary, at least strong supervisory input from the instructor is provided. This input should consist of three core steps:

1. guidance toward and approval of the topic;
2. review of sources to be used (if necessary, depending on the topic), which also means being able to attest the necessity of dubious material; and
3. taking necessary steps to ensure that the end result is only used for academic purposes.

In this way, at least some safeguards are introduced but without excessive bureaucratic burdens.

CONCLUSION

This chapter demonstrates the practical and ethical benefits of designing offensive influence campaigns when teaching a module on information security. It has been shown that, due to the specificity of the subject, any claim to an objective position from which one could teach an uninfluenced truth is highly problematic. It is also more likely that there will be highly diverse truth claims within the class. Hence, attempts to find a common frame of reference should be abandoned.

Instead of aiming for some synthesis, diversity of views should be embraced. Allowing students to create their own fictional psyops does not require the students to have identical perceptions of their environment. Hence, conflicts of interpretation are avoided; moreover, the students who do not conform to the majority or the instructor's worldview are spared the stigma of being labeled manipulated automatons rather than autonomous subjects. It seems more likely that such stigmatization would adversely affect their willingness to participate and to take away anything meaningful from the class.

Finally, the instructor no longer has to adopt the impossible position of somebody who is above ambiguity and "false consciousness" (the alternative would be the hypocrisy of someone who is aware of his or her own partiality but still presents it as universality). Instead, the ethically preferable stance is to acknowledge one's own fallibility as well as that of others. At the same time, the presence of clear marking criteria based on technique and process does preclude complete "anything goes" relativism.

Chapter Eight

Touchy Subjects

Utilizing Handedness as a Precursor to Discussing Privilege and Diversity in the Classroom

Bryan L. Dawson

The University of North Georgia is home to many psychology students who seek to use their education to advance their careers. Many of these students, however, have not had meaningful experiences with other cultures outside their immediate surrounding area. This chapter focuses on one promising way to foster culturally competent students who appreciate diversity and analyze their experiences in discussing topics that have been traditionally "glossed over" in university classrooms. This chapter describes the practical applications of Peggy McIntosh's (1993) idea of the "invisible knapsack" to discuss issues of privilege, building on small differences, such as handedness, and moving on to gender disparities, age differences, and ethnic perceptions among predominantly white students in the southern United States, while at the same time fostering a safe classroom environment to analyze these issues. It focuses on several activities to develop sensitivity to diversity in a semester-long Organizational Behavior course. Similar activities can be used in other undergraduate courses exploring the issues of diversity.

Using the metaphor of an invisible knapsack, McIntosh (1993) relates her experiences as a white woman and the unearned resources she has been given due to her ethnicity and emphasizes that privileges and resources are not distributed equally among different ethnicities or genders. McIntosh's work is helpful for educators working in diverse classrooms and teaching about difference due to its clarity and the author's ability to relate everyday activities to issues of privilege. Undergraduate students can understand and appreciate her argument. McIntosh illustrates white privilege: "I can easily buy posters, post-cards, picture books, greeting cards, dolls, toys and children's magazines featuring people of my race" (1993, 33). Members of other races, by contrast, may have difficulty finding such things. Students can begin to understand the phenomenon of privilege when they see it illustrated in such examples.

It is easy to think of various identities (e.g., gender, race, culture) as entirely separate categories, but in fact, these identities intersect to create unique combinations. For example, instructors can ask their students to think of themselves not simply based on their gender and to move toward a more inclusive understanding of multiple identities and the unique and complicated challenges and privileges that may come from these identities. It is important to understand the intersectionality of identities as arising from multiple sources so that students do not limit themselves to thinking of identity in reductionist terms.

In an Organizational Behavior course, for example, the instructor covers many topics dealing with the workplace as these relate to psychology, including performance appraisal, selecting employees, motivation, promotion, leadership, diversity, and inclusion through lecture and discussion. The main goal of such a course is to familiarize students with industrial-organizational psychology and the mechanisms surrounding psychology in the workplace.

An Organizational Behavior course offers a good opportunity to familiarize students with the impact of privilege on the organizations in which people work. The instructor may set aside time in both lecture and discussion settings to specifically address issues of harassment, discrimination, and microaggressions (Hyde 1998; Remer and Remer 2000; Sue et al. 2007) as they may exist in today's heterogeneous workplace. Through lecture and structured discussion framework, students are presented with the relevant literature and information first and then given the opportunity to share their insights and reflections concerning their initial assumptions and their newfound understanding, as well as provided with the opportunity to experience other viewpoints beyond their own experience (Ferdman 2003b). Bernardo M. Ferdman (2003b) suggests that such a framework is integral to broaching issues of inclusion and diversity because such a structure allows all parties to have a shared knowledge base, gain rapport with fellow students, and develop a deeper understanding of their perspectives.

PRIVILEGE AS A PRECURSOR TO INCLUSION

Peggy McIntosh (1993) discusses the issues of privilege as an invisible knapsack that affords individuals certain special provisions and advantages that they have not necessarily earned. Privilege may be based on gender, race, nationality, or religion, among others, but at its core reflects systemic advantages afforded to an individual based on membership to a group (e.g., being white or being female). Through becoming aware of one's own personal privileges, it is possible to begin to understand the unearned disadvantages that others may face.

It is important, however, to relate this information in a manner that does not blame individuals for their privilege or assign fault for societal privileges but rather to question the validity of privilege and its origin. Through a better understanding of invisible advantages, students may begin to more effectively comprehend and recognize the disadvantages others may experience.

Furthermore, Kecia M. Thomas, Ny M. Tran, and Bryan L. Dawson (2011) discuss the use of privilege as a method of exploring individual earned advantages and disadvantages while allowing groups who may view themselves as different (e.g., black women and white men) to see some common ground in their possible combined heterosexual privilege, even though they may differ in their gender and racial experiences. They suggest that, through group exploration of privileges that exist beyond the individual, participants may be able to better understand the benefits of an inclusive multicultural framework on which to build.

In other words, realizing that the benefit of being heterosexual may have unintended consequences for others who do not identify as such within the workplace allows an individual to begin to comprehend the disadvantages that their LGBTQ coworkers may face. Moving toward an inclusive environment enables a person to deconstruct these issues of privilege, thereby granting all groups a more equal footing. If an individual remains unaware of the invisible advantages he or she is afforded, the person may be less inclined to seek out and advocate changing the status quo within the workplace or societal environment.

ADDRESSING PRIVILEGE IN A CLASSROOM ENVIRONMENT

Addressing issues of privilege among a majority group can be a difficult task. Some research has suggested that, if handled improperly, discussing privilege has the potential for catastrophic backlash from students, especially if they feel that they are being targeted for an unjust system, which may lead to more negative climate for diversity (Dawson and Goren 2011; Hite and McDonald 2006; Schmidt 2004). Using handedness as an introduction to privilege in the classroom may help the students to articulate the feelings of what it is like to be different from their peers. Left- or right-handedness turns out to be a useful heuristic device for discussing the question of privilege that students can understand. Typically, there will be one or two left-handed students in a class. Handedness is one of the things many people who are right-handed never even consider in their daily lives. Left-handed individuals, roughly 10 percent of the population, are presented with a predominantly right-handed world (Papadatou-Pastou et al. 2008).

It may be useful to begin the exercise by asking students who are left-handed to identify themselves. Then ask the right-handed students what some of the stereotypes they have heard about left-handed people entail. This results in typical responses, such as "Left-handed people are evil" followed by chuckling, "Left-handed people have sloppy handwriting," "Left-handed people are really creative," or the ever-prevalent "Left-handed people need special scissors." Next, ask the left-handed students to discuss whether they believe there is any truth to these statements. Obviously, left-handed people are not evil, but it is a prevalent myth in our society that the left hand is evil. For instance, the Latin word *sinistra* means "left" and "unlucky" and is the root of our English word *sinister*. Furthermore, in French, *gauche* means both "left" and "clumsy," whereas *droit* means both "right" and "straight." A Google search for "left hand evil" pulls up the Wikipedia article "Bias against left-handed people" as the first result, accompanied by some 59.9 million results.

While not evil or clumsy, left-handed students can get very defensive over the sloppy handwriting issue. Left-handed students often say that their handwriting may appear sloppy, but that it is due to the world being made for right-handed people. For example, notebooks (especially spiral bound) are designed for right-handed use only. This begins a discussion in which the left-handed students identify how they are disadvantaged in life. Many students express their unfortunate experiences opening doors (which are usually designed to be opened with the right hand) and their coping mechanisms for reaching around and being blamed for bumping elbows with right-handed people during dinner and coping by sitting on the outside of a table or booth, even if it is not their preferred seating choice, and being forced to get up any time someone has to get out to use the restroom. In the past, some left-handed students expressed their frustration with having to carry hand sanitizer as a method of removing ink stains from their palms due to notebooks made for right-handed writers. Others have even experienced educational delays by being held back a year as elementary school teachers tried to force them to become right-handed. During this time, many of the right-handed students express shock. Ink smudges, being relegated to the end of table, and especially being held back in school were issues that never crossed their minds as being related to such a trivial matter as left-handedness. Through the left-handed students' personal experiences, right-handed students are exposed to the unearned disadvantages their classmates must contend with. Utilizing handedness as an icebreaker for privilege allows the students to reflect on their own unearned advantages of being right-handed and begin to better understand the true difficulties of being left-handed in a right-handed world.

During this time, it is important to remind the students that it is not their fault that the world is fashioned for right-handed ease of use but that it is something that continues. The right-handed students then are asked to think of their unearned privileges in light of the new information. After some careful thought, students have responded, "Right-handed people never have to worry about an inky handshake jeopardizing their job interview," "Right-handed people can choose where they sit in class beyond one of the few desks that support left-handed writing," or "Right-handed people can buy sporting equipment more easily." Right-handed students invariably ask, "Why don't they make notebooks for left-handed people?" to which the left-handed students reply, "They do; they are just considerably more expensive, and we have to pay for them." Similar exchanges in class serve to illustrate a few key points. First, privileged individuals are generally unaware of the disadvantages their counterparts face. Second, upon becoming aware, they are more likely to question the unfair system and seek answers. Third, upon realizing their privileges and their counterparts' perceptions, people with privileges start to value those advantages more than before.

AWARENESS CREATION

While addressing issues of privilege can be a helpful starting point for diversity awareness, it cannot be used alone to adequately address inclusion and diversity in the workplace. An instructor can use his or her own privileges of being heterosexual, male, or middle-class to ease students into the deeper subjects of race, sexual orientation, and gender. Diversity trainers are most effective when they are knowledgeable about their own identities, privileges, and biases (Bussema and Nemec 2006; Kitzinger and Peel 2005).

The course can analyze how to integrate diversity awareness into such practices as selection and performance appraisals, as well as the development of biases. It is important that students understand that these biases may be due to prejudices or misattributions arising from stereotypes that individuals possess. By learning about their own identities, individuals lay the foundation for learning about the identities of others and how these "others" may share similar characteristics with them (Ferdman 2003b). By starting from a broad view of diversity in the classroom, the instructor can start building awareness of differences in every community, including this class (e.g., differences exist, even in handedness). The next step is to start developing a narrower focus on specific categories and tie them to concrete aspects of the workplace (e.g., performance appraisals, promotions, leadership development (Chrobot-Mason 2004; Griswold et al. 2007; Gutiérrez et al. 2000).

When discussing issues related to power and privilege, it is important for students to be able to discuss the disadvantages that accompany power and privilege as well. This allows all students to realize that, while they have some unearned advantages, they are not simply select individuals who have it easy. Doing so also helps to minimize backlash from students in discussing privilege. By discussing both privileges and disadvantages, the instructor can demonstrate that privilege is not a targeting mechanism and emphasize that people from all backgrounds can strive for improvement of the human condition.

Given that many of these students are discussing such difficult issues for the first time, it is useful to focus on assessing student understanding and learning by using Donald L. Kirkpatrick's "Four-Level Learning Evaluation Model" (1959), which focuses on:

1. *The Reaction of the Students*: Did the learners like the process?
2. *Student Learning*: How much knowledge was gained?
3. *Student Behavior*: Did the learning process result in changes?
4. *Results*: What are the tangible results of the learning process?

Level 1 is typically assessed informally through class discussion. It is possible to include relevant examination questions as well.

Level 2 is assessed by the formal exam and essay questions. For example, the instructor could ask the students to discuss the topic that they feel could help them most in their future careers. If the exercise on "handedness" was successful, then it is likely to be remembered by the students during the exam. In addition, they can choose to incorporate additional readings and the ways in which they plan to integrate sensitivity to diversity into their daily lives.

It is difficult to conceptualize levels 3 and 4 because it is not possible to keep track of all students who took the class to ensure that changes in their thinking persist over time. Some information can be gathered from the students who keep in touch with the professor and discuss their experiences in organizations with him or her.

Allowing students to discuss their own beliefs in semiprivate discussions during the early stages in the course enables them to practice their cultural competencies and demonstrate what they have learned. Others have also discussed the importance of allowing students to draw on their own experiences and reflect on their potential biases and challenges (Kirk and Durant 2010).

Students can work on their own definitions of *inclusion* as it pertains to a workplace environment and are encouraged to discuss their experiences from their current and past employment as the class moves into issues related to gender biases and race. This provides a voice to these group members, as many students realize their experiences are not singular but shared across multiple students, and allows these students to feel their issues are being recognized (Kulik et al. 2007).

The class can brainstorm and look for ways to move beyond these biases and to consider which issues are reinforcing these biases, both within the organizational climate and our societal expectations of certain groups. Discussing diversity after these exercises and self-reflection become a transformative experience for some students. While brainstorming, students continue to come back to the notion of awareness as it pertains to themselves, their perceptions, and their interpretations of their own actions and of the actions of others. Awareness is a fundamental skill that must be learned for true progress to begin in appreciating diversity (Kirk and Durant 2010).

Students can then discuss the strategies of inclusion in organizations that extend beyond mandatory training, employee luncheons, and cultural competency training. Tying training to promotion and recognizing the benefits for organizations, such as additional mentoring opportunities for traditionally devalued groups and better intergroup communication and retention of minority employees, are matters students often acknowledge in such discussions (Chrobot-Mason 2004; C. Lee and Chon 2000).

The next step is to ask the students to create mock guidelines for organizations to develop and incorporate inclusive practices. During this time, the class can also discuss microaggressions (brief and common verbal or behavioral assaults or insults that serve to invalidate or undermine someone of a different ethnicity or gender) and the lasting impact of dealing with these issues for targets of discrimination (Sue et al. 2007). Students have particularly expressed great interest in this issue, as it gave them a term for experiences they had but felt unable to express.

TYING EXPERIENCE TO REAL-WORLD ORGANIZATIONS

Finally, students examine selected real-world organizations and their commitments to diversity through mass media, organizational websites, third-party sources, and the law. In addition, the students develop potential training exercises to help all individuals to feel comfortable and safe discussing differences in organizational settings, particularly as they pertain to leaders who may look different from them (see Rosette, Leonardelli, and Phillips 2008). A common theme throughout the course is relating material back to real-world situations and experiences. Through this exposure to relevant theoretical reviews, classroom application, and research on a current organization's practice of inclusion and diversity, students are immersed in practicing inclusion in the classroom (Ferdman 2010).

Students write a group paper on their chosen institution's organizational philosophies and diversity initiatives, as well as a short personal reaction paper addressing their own perceptions of how a real-world organization that they have researched approached diversity and what aspects of these approaches they would like to see in their future employers. During the final week of the course, students present their findings regarding the diversity initiatives to their classmates. In addition, they offer their own evaluations of their researched organizations using the material covered throughout the semester.

CONCLUSION

Instructors teaching various subjects may utilize the methods presented here to incorporate the touchy subjects of diversity and inclusion into their classrooms, especially when faced with a demographic that, at first glance, may not be very receptive to addressing these topics. People are more than they appear to be on the surface. Skin color, gender, age, and similar categories are only some aspects of the identities of individuals. Student feedback has shown that the presented strategies allow students to explore aspects of themselves and others in a safe and informative setting, knowledge that they can bring with them later into the workplace.

Chapter Nine

Favorite Place Mapmaking and the Decolonization of Teaching

Barbara Tedrow

This chapter explains a teaching strategy called "sense of place mapmaking" that can decolonize teaching, or get rid of hierarchical teaching from one viewpoint that values facts, not imagination. This chapter is based on experiences in two classrooms in South Africa and the United States teaching first-year college students who were preparing to serve as student teachers. Mapmaking lets student teachers use teaching practices from many disciplines, such as geography, geology, history, and environmental and political sciences, to uncover the physical features of place and connect them to the social context of a favorite place. The processes depicted in this chapter helped the students to identify and communicate their favorite places with their unique features in a personal and objective way for others to see and understand. Mapmaking can be an effective teaching method in community building and critical thinking in various disciplines, not only education.

David Sobel's (1998) book on "sense of place" education raises an important question: Why do most schools overlook a student's life experience as a starting point for teaching? Interest in this question originated with the author's background as a first-generation college student from an Eastern European family who were employed in the United States as coal miners. The stereotypes of working-class coal miners often depicted the group as primitive and uneducated.

In the United States, climbing the ladder means fitting in and working hard. But it is impossible to escape the influences of time and place because "fitting in" does not happen in the same way in all contexts (Jefferson 2015). Historical experiences (such as colonialism) can play an important role in similar processes.

Social class issues have remained taboo in former colonial countries and in the countries where outside powers dominated indigenous groups and countries with large immigrant populations. Students from such backgrounds often endured daily subtle verbal and behavioral indignities about religious differences, backwardness that equated to lack of intelligence, accents, odd-sounding last names, and child-rearing practices. Such experiences create anxiety and shame (Law 1995, 1–3). Researchers emphasize that a student's concentration and ability to learn is inhibited by such negative emotions as fear, anxiety, and shame (Brackett and Rivers 2014; Sue et al. 2009). Carola Suárez-Orozco and others found that black and Hispanic students today suffer from similar consequences due to subtle assaults on their identities (2015, 151–60).

Society's solution should be not to change students to fit in but to transform societal structures so that they can become "beings for themselves." The banking or depositing system of learning, also known as traditional learning, does not teach students about their context and its influence on sense of self. English remains the primary language of learning in many multiethnic areas today that were once under colonialism (Pennycock 2013). It is logical to assume that many students, especially minorities, feel marginalized in such situations. From this background, the question becomes, How do teachers decolonize their teaching for the good of all students?

Sobel's (1998) work on mapmaking and sense of place includes lessons to teach schoolchildren about their connection to geography, history, and their environment. He argues that his approach is a "natural fit" for all children because, in early developmental phases, children explore geographical boundaries. Sobel's reference to early developmental learning supports adult mapmaking because the mapmaking idea decolonizes teaching practices by empowering those who feel that they belong to a "nonmainstream" group to see the influences to their sense of self. Drawing maps of a favorite place using one of several viewpoints, like a pictorial (flat, one-dimensional), panoramic (two-dimensional), or aerial (top-down view), helps to enlarge memory of the place's elements, such as the land contour, vegetation, boundaries, wildlife, people, and events, that interface with the students' physical spaces, showing relative spatial relationships.

Positive responses by the students in the United States and South Africa to such teaching included the following:

"Though I saw my favorite geographical place often through my life, after teaching mapmaking I was able to see with deeper clarity my connection to nature. I didn't think I could draw or even write. Now I see that I can use research, drawing, and writing to communicate my experience about how I can learn from nature."—A student from the United States

"Factual reporting of my place took on more detail when I first wrote the descriptions in my mother tongue because the mother tongue sounds were a part of the memory of my place. This technique opened many new ways of learning from nature, so many that I knew this was how we could begin to teach students to understand their world and their place in it."—A student from South Africa

MAPMAKING AND ESSAY WRITING WORK TOGETHER

The Favorite Place Mapmaking Project invites a student to remember a personal favorite place in nature, such as under the maple tree at their grandfather's house where they played in sand or the summer cottage where the dolphins swam or the walk down a dirt mountain road. Then students are encouraged to explore the elements of the favorite place, such as climate, land contours, forests, wildlife, vegetation, sounds, ponds, people, and routes of transportation. The students are asked to draw a map of the place and include the elements of the place that creates their emotional connection with a story of their experience.

The students can try all three perspectives but should choose one for the final large map: draw the favorite place from a pictorial (front view), panoramic (wide view), or aerial view (top view). The map will include symbolic as well as representations distinct to the students' experiences of place. Researching the mapmaking project enhances the students' awareness of their personal connections to geography, geology, history, vegetation, and events.

In addition, research and mapping help to piece together the students' understanding of their emotional connections to the places that are mapped. This greater awareness can lead to an understanding of commonalities rather than the stark differences. For example, the contours of a particular geographical place may be different for each student, but feelings of aloneness, sadness, confusion, or homesickness linked to a place can emerge as a commonality.

THE MAPMAKING METHOD

Mapmaking can be taught in a traditional semester course framework (about ten weeks long) as a self-directed project, with four assignments organized in a take-home packet. The packet contains four assignment sheets with goals, deadline policies, rules for participation, and grading standards if used in a credit course.

The four mapmaking assignments are:

1. map drawing—from first sketches to final draft;

2. physically measuring the boundaries of the student's identified place with a "pacing" formula;
3. collecting data via Internet, interviews, and observation with a double-entry data sheet that also records the student's personal awareness; and
4. constructing an outline, writing an essay, and presenting the final map.

The course can be taught in three sessions, each about sixty to ninety minutes long. In session 1, the instructor introduces the general concept of map drawing, which includes directions for the initial sketches of place, identifies the three map perspectives (front view, panoramic view, and aerial view), and the final large color map image drawn on a poster board.

The second assignment in the take-home packet presented in session 1 is about research and investigative techniques. Pace-length, a measuring technique, is a way to codify the area and perimeter of a place based on the student's walking step. The students measure their step or pace length with a yard stick or tape measure and then translate that into inches, feet, or the metric equivalent. The pace-length code is used to report a place's area and perimeter.

The second assignment in session 1 continues by explaining how to gather data and organize research notes with a double-entry data sheet, with factual information on the top half and personal reflections on the bottom half. For example, if students choose to identify vegetation by using online tools, then the students identify the plant and describe it (dried and flattened plants can be pasted to this section). On the bottom half of sheet, the students might explain their personal connections to a tree, poison ivy, or type of mushrooms picked at this place. The findings part of the investigative process gives texture and specific detail to the outline, map, essay, or oral story.

Session 1 sets the expectation that no one's beliefs, art, and culture will be mocked. This is challenging because students can intimidate other students subtly outside of class, causing participation anxiety. Adequate time must be given to developing sensitivity to individual customs and traditions.

Session 2, generally held around midterm, is devoted to the essay assignment and questions related to the writing process. This session discusses outlining and connecting the findings to the students' experiences in writing. With adult students or mature writers, the teacher may assign chapters from William Knowlton Zinsser's *Writing to Learn* (2006) or Robin Hemley's *A Field Guide for Immersion Writing: Memoir, Journalism, and Travel* (2015) as background reading prior to developing the essay or outline for the story.

Session 3, scheduled near the end of the semester, gives the students the opportunity to share the final drafts of their maps, tell their stories using the prepared outlines, and submit the essays to the teacher with such collected data as interview notes and the double-entry data sheets. The students can also include references to previously published works about the place; for example, the history of a particular county related to their place. Alternatively, they may include informal interview summaries from people who know of the place or with similar experiences.

Students are not expected to visualize their maps or write about them without first viewing several completed maps and essays. The teacher's map is the prototype of favorite place mapmaking. Using a large sheet of medium-weight poster board, the teacher shows an example of his or her favorite place image as a small place from a larger context in a colorful image. Teachers may refer to maps from books, such as "100 Aker Wood" from *Winnie-the-Pooh* (Milne 2014), *Treasure Island* (Stevenson 1993), *My Father's Dragon* (Gannett 1948), and *The Hobbit* (Tolkien 1966) to illustrate the visual organization of a place.

Mapmaking is an effective teaching tool because, when teaching geography and social studies, mapping is a way for students to immerse themselves in a location, connecting with such elements as people, roads, houses, prominent trees and flowers, wildlife, climate, contours, and events. The pictorial, aerial, or panoramic map can spatially connect a place's specific elements with the student's feeling of the chosen place.

There is potential to advance the discussion about what the student believes needs to be done to protect the location from deterioration and its connection to the larger issue of sustainable development. This can be a basis for subsequent service learning projects. Mapmaking for the decolonization of teaching practices takes preparation and planning. Ultimately, the success of mapmaking rests on the teacher's leadership and students' trust, as well as student-to-student trust and collaboration.

The students could be asked to write a five-hundred-word essay that tells the story of their maps. The essay content should contrast the student's memory of their favorite place with present details. For example, the students could also describe their places as insiders and then as outsiders, noting the changes in their perspectives of the natural settings and their personal responses to the changes caused by such events as war, famine, modernization, and other events meaningful to them.

The contrast between memory and reality provides a backdrop to the notion of sustaining nature as more people populate or depopulate the student's place. During the story writing, such concepts as geography, mapping, family relationships, history, literature, politics, and science can provide connections for understanding emerging complex questions. The essay assignment can be negotiated with student writing partners to listen to drafts and help with editing.

At the last session (session 3), the students share their maps and stories and are given the opportunity to tell what they would like to learn more about. They may bring an artifact from the place that prompts memories, such as shoes that they wore at the place or a soil sample. The students' experiences generally build on their commonalities, such as the need to belong and the pain of isolation. A conference session with each student may be necessary to ensure the student is meeting the goals of the assignment.

Students could be assigned sample essays to help them to write their own favorite place essays. For example, a Georgia State University student wrote about her favorite place, Molasses Beach:

> My special place is a coral reef off the island of Key Largo, Florida. It is approximately one mile off shore, and it's an underwater paradise. I discovered the reef at the age of twelve when I went snorkeling with a friend. Expecting the usual coral and sea weed, I was not prepared for what I actually found: a brightly colored bed of coral and sea fans brimming with all kinds of sea life. Sharks, rays, lobster, sea urchins, and barracuda are just a few of its many inhabitants. I have always been very comfortable in the ocean, having grown up in the Keys.

The favorite place can be one prism to understand self and others as the students discover how similarities and differences come together to create commonalities between them and other students. This is important because students live in a fast-paced world of competition and education is often not designed to build community but to provide workplace skills. Thus, most individuals are forced to ignore similarities and clutch to differences and do not develop a vocabulary to describe their surroundings that helps to interact with others easily.

FAVORITE PLACE MAPMAKING PROJECT: SOUTH AFRICA

I was offered a Fulbright Specialist Grant to pursue teaching via mapmaking in South Africa. As the instructor prepared for the course, the question asked in the beginning of this chapter came up once more: Why do most schools overlook a student's place and life experience as a starting point for teaching and learning when it seems like such a natural starting point? South Africa adopted one of the most advanced constitutions in the world to ensure justice and equality in their multicultural society. How would their colonial-type educational system be affected by a new participatory government?

However, in education, the inclusive changes were not universally embraced because some politically powerful factions worried that such inclusiveness would lower the educational quality (Tedrow and Mabokela 2006). Alternative, smaller-scale assignments were used to promote inclusiveness. The goal was to experiment with mapmaking to discover whether, as a teaching method, it would build bridges between different groups by exploring the idea of a "favorite place." Workshops in two universities in the Eastern Cape of South Africa organized the participating students into groups of twenty to twenty-five people. The students defined their favorite places, drew their maps at home, did some basic research, and told their stories in two ninety-minute class sessions three days apart.

In the South Africa context, the favorite place project connected to "graphicacy." *Graphicacy* is defined as the visualizing of reasoning data in a graph and identified as a literacy standard in South Africa and Europe. In this project, word graphs and timelines could be used, but it also introduced a notion of a visualized map of a geographical location with its various elements. As a result, graphicacy, geography, and social learning for a sustainable environment interfaced (Sterling 2007). The essay requirement was revised. This was necessary because, in 2008, South Africa had eleven official languages, and many indigenous students could speak English, but they had limited ability to read and write it well. The Favorite Place Mapmaking Project supported teacher-preparation students and adult teachers who were being retrained for teaching in a democratic country.

For the most part, the students enthusiastically embraced the mapmaking idea; eagerly assembled the stories of their favorite places; and presented them to each other, sharing their sense of belonging, love of a particular work associated with the land, and how it fostered relationships with their families. What surfaced in the mapmaking assignments were stories of fun and loss, as when a family divorced or the student never returned to their vacation house because it was too dangerous to visit given the level of unrest during the transition from apartheid. Some thought of ways to save the natural settings of their places by organizing the community for a clean-up. Others told of their stories as refugees from other African countries and their sense of isolation.

One student's favorite place was the apple orchard owned by a white farmer. Though forbidden by his parents, the student found it a great game to swim the creek to get to the orchard and outwit the farmer by picking the apples without being caught. What ensued in class was a discussion about private ownership, definition of theft, and if the student's desire for a challenge or the need for apples could have been channeled in another way to foster good relations with his neighbor.

Mapmaking piqued urban students' interest in visiting the townships near their college town that they had only passed in cars because the townships were perceived as dangerous territory. One professor in South Africa who organized a field trip took her students atop a high cliff on the edge of town to view the college and the surrounding community. The students saw a real panoramic map of the divisions between the rich and poor, with elegant two-story homes a few miles from smaller township homes and then a descent to temporary settlements. A few days later, the teacher took students to visit a township and a township school that they would have not visited previously.

From these shared stories, it became clear that the mapmaking project could be an important bridge-builder as well as a change agent.

The mapmaking assignment enables the teacher and the student flexibility to adjust assignments to meet student needs, levels of understanding, and language abilities. Students may need time to build an outline and then adjust for a coherent narrative before the writing of their essays. Given an opportunity to write in their mother tongue in a multilingual classroom in South Africa, the students liked the descriptions they could give that were not possible in their limited use of English. Some teachers allowed time for the essay to be written in the student's mother tongue and in English, providing assistance to present the map to a multicultural audience.

CONCLUSION

The Favorite Place Mapmaking Project can be useful in many different contexts because many modern educational systems are built on the legacy of colonial education. The project may be time-consuming at first, and flexibility will be needed to allow adequate time for drawing, writing, and sharing. Favorite place mapmaking has the potential to challenge traditional teaching philosophies that limit the right of the students to know themselves and their cultural worlds while balancing that with teaching scientific factual data of the modern world.

Was there a downside to the project? In both countries, the teachers felt overburdened with changes and expectations of their governments for specific measurable assessment standards. Moreover, students who were successful in memorization tests were hesitant to embark on this new type of learning and tell about themselves. "Sense of place" teaching allowed students to appreciate cultural differences and similarities, but some did not see these insights as important because education continued to be perceived as a series of certificates needed for employment that did not include a complex journey of self-discovery in a social context.

Students who participated in the Favorite Place Mapmaking Project learned how "sense of place" activities support learning and an understanding of self and their world. This understanding is important for all students but especially for those with multicultural backgrounds.

Chapter Ten

Making Strangers of Ourselves

*Role-Playing the Immigrant Experience in a
College Classroom*

Ellen G. Rafshoon

This chapter begins with an explanation of why immigration history is emphasized within a survey class. It demonstrates how traditional approaches, such as lecturing based on textbook information, are inadequate. If an instructor organizes her syllabus according to the topics in the typical U.S. history survey text, then migration and ethnicity will be tangential. Students will end the semester failing to comprehend how the origins of America's remarkable multiculturalism formed the country. They will also lack exposure to the basic knowledge and skills that are essential for successful participation in diverse contexts, whether at home or abroad.

In the second part of the chapter, an innovative interdisciplinary approach used to teach this subject is detailed. Students begin by reading Anzia Yezierska's *Bread Givers* (1975; originally published in 1925). This novel is a Polish-Jewish equivalent of Jane Austen's *Pride and Prejudice* (2014; originally published in 1813), which relates the efforts of the family patriarch to marry off his four daughters to wealthy men after arriving in New York. Yezierska patterns the rebellious youngest daughter after herself; other characters are also derived from her dramatic life. Thus, for pedagogical purposes, the novel functions as both a work of literature and a historical primary source (Dearborn 1988).

Because experiential learning techniques are considered the most effective in cultivating empathy for those who are considered strangers, role-playing is the centerpiece of the exercise (Foster 1999; Gerdes et al. 2011). Each student adopts the persona of a character in Yezierska's book and writes an essay from his or her character's perspective. The final component is a structured classroom discussion, where students continue to inhabit their immigrant personas. Using the intersectional approach, students see that an immigrant's adaptation to American life varies from group to group and individual to individual because the experience is affected by notions of identity. An intersectional analysis is also useful because it stresses the contingent nature of identity—that salient features, such as race, gender, and class, function differently depending on the context (Ferdman 2003b).

Yezierska's novel is acute in its illustration of the complexity of identity, especially in its exploration of how gender roles affect an immigrant's experience. The immigrants portrayed in the novel are poor Russian Jews, whose rituals and customs enforce a strict patriarchy. Their gender and religious norms conflict with American ones, putting enormous strain on the family unit. There is no happy ending to their story; even the protagonist, who achieves professional success, perceives she has lost valuable parts of her identity in becoming American.

WHERE TRADITIONAL APPROACHES FALL SHORT

"Once I thought to write a history of the immigrants in America. Then I discovered that the immigrants *were* American history." These are the famous first sentences of Oscar Handlin's Pulitzer Prize–winning book *The Uprooted: The Epic Story of the Great Migrations That Made the American People* (1951). As the opening of *The Uprooted* makes clear, the movement of foreigners to the United States was (and is) central to the development of the United States. But what made Handlin's work path-breaking when it was published sixty years ago was that he sought to capture the inner life of an immigrant.

With evidence culled from poignant letters and diary entries, Handlin concludes that most immigrants suffered from alienation, even as they contributed mightily to strengthening democracy in America. At his death in 2010 at ninety-five, Handlin was recalled as having inspired the field of immigration studies, which uses the tools of sociology, psychology, and history to provide nuanced portraits of immigrants and their communities.

One of the strongest explanations for the existing neglect of immigration in history education at all levels is the persistence of the debatable "melting pot" paradigm, which presumes that foreigners strive to assimilate and do so successfully by the second generation (Archdeacon 1985). When the paradigm is applied to interpret America's past, the ethnic origins of groups or individuals have limited relevance for the immigrants or the nation as a whole. Despite efforts to discredit the "melting pot" analogy, it nonetheless exerts a powerful force for those who see education as a means of building national unity and instilling patriotism.

A recent study of state guidelines for teaching immigration in middle and high schools demonstrates that there are two extremes in the nation's classrooms. On the one hand, students are taught that newcomers contribute to the cohesive "social fabric" or "melting pot." On the other hand, they learn a lot about how immigrants stand apart as "others" because a good deal of high school instruction centers on xenophobic policies. Unfortunately, references to hostile reactions toward newcomers take the lion's share of coverage in public high schools rather than instances of how individuals from diverse ethnic backgrounds have enriched American life. The impression one gets is that immigrants are "burdensome to American society" (Journell 2009).

Besides depicting immigrants as a drain on national resources, rarely are immigrants depicted as active participants in their own destinies, according to Journell (2009). In many states, the story recounted in secondary school classrooms begins with an immigrant's flight from the Old World and ends with his arrival at Ellis Island. Ignored is the "difficult cultural adjustment that many groups faced" afterward.

Because the story of immigration does not move forward in time to the post–World War II era, high school students are not instructed about why the national quota laws were overturned in 1965 to permit the influx of millions of Latin Americans, Asians, and Africans—the parents of many of today's students. The state of Georgia, where I teach, has seen the proportion of foreign-born residents grow from 2.7 percent to 9.7 percent in the last two decades (1990–2014). It ranks at the bottom in teaching any aspects of immigration (Journell 2009; Migration Policy Institute n.d.).

Regrettably, a student entering college would not find a richer treatment of immigration than she experienced in high school if the only U.S. history course she takes is the required survey (Vecchio 2004). Popular textbooks are generally lackluster in their approach to immigration and ethnicity (Boyer et al. 2011; Foner 2011; Roark et al. 2011). Because the main events covered in American history texts occur at polling places and battlefields, places seemingly irrelevant to immigrant life, this minimizes coverage of the topic. Unless immigrants are directly involved in an event, they are not going to be mentioned as important historical figures. Rather, college survey texts relate immigration as distinct to certain eras, usually having to do with the arrival of masses of foreigners on American shores (Vecchio 2004).

Their newfound presence of foreigners is unwittingly linked to negative consequences, such as urban squalor, competition for jobs, and labor and social unrest. As in high school instruction, there is a lack of information on the post-1965 migrations. For example, the typical college textbook mentions Ellis and Angel Islands but rarely cites recent gateways, such as JFK and Miami International Airports and border crossings at San Ysidro, California, and Laredo, Texas—the busiest in the world. These are where today's students or their parents likely first set foot on American soil.

Also problematic in college texts are references to transplanted Americans exclusively by their national origins, such as the Slavs, Irish, or Mexicans. This characterization reduces immigrant groups to formless masses, another roadblock for teaching students to empathize with the immigrant experience. One historian has remarked that the sole use of national designations undermines a more accurate portrait of immigrant life, which inhabits "small worlds of family and community bonds" (Radzilowski 2009). In addition, defining immigrants by their birthplaces presumes a "within group homogeneity" that may not be present in class, religious, or gender distinctions.

SETTING THE STAGE

The lived experience of immigrants is emphasized in the course offered here as an alternative. This, after all, is what the history discipline prizes; namely, the ability to see events from the viewpoints of past actors to gain insight into the cultural, economic, and political arrangements of their time. If the students walk in the shoes of these people, then perhaps they can grasp how they perceived the enormity of the changes unfolding around these people and their role as agents of those changes.

Did women face different challenges and have different aspirations than men? Who seemed to benefit from the move, the old or the young? What did they think it meant to be an American? If you remained poor after many years in the "promised land," then could the move be considered a success? How did the larger culture and society respond to immigrants in the short and long term? Are immigrants in the past different from or similar to today's migrants? These are some of the many questions that students should be prompted to consider. Of course, all of this is designed to help today's students to make sense of the present. The current cohort of college graduates is expected to communicate and collaborate in diverse cultural and international contexts. To do this successfully, they must be able to develop what one multicultural educator describes as an "other-oriented perspective congruent with another's sociocultural values, political ideology, and historical context" (Louie 2005).

Before students delve into Yezierska's novel, they are provided with a thorough grounding in the terms and categories of analysis that are used to make sense of the characters' behavior. Students first listen to a lecture that begins by asking them to consider Handlin's perspective on the centrality of immigration to American history. Students learn why the professor finds Handlin's perspective compelling and how they will discuss the impact of immigration and ethnicity on U.S. history when the unit on the topic is complete. The presentation includes an introduction to integral sociological and legal vocabulary, such as *pull* and *push*, *refugee*, *naturalization*, and *nativism*. There is an explanation of the myriad ways one obtains permission to move to the United States and how entry requirements have changed over time.

Because the U.S. Census Bureau is a vital source for immigration data, the history and constitutional mandate of the bureau is explained, along with information on how the racial and ethnic categories to classify Americans have changed over time. One set of statistics that always interests the students is a table showing the billions of dollars that immigrants generate in the form of "remittances" to top sending nations, such as Mexico, India, and the Philippines (World Bank 2015). This data places the study of immigration within a transnational context and demonstrates how migration remains integral to the world economy.

A second lecture validates *Bread Givers* as a historical source and situates the students in Yezierska's world before they start reading the book. While the novel's plot and characters are fictional, Yezierska's work nevertheless has credibility as a primary source of historical understanding. The author uses her imagined characters to reveal her firsthand knowledge of what it was like to be an Eastern European female coming of age in early-twentieth-century America. Some literary experts believe that Yezierska's fiction was actually more truthful than her autobiography, *Red Ribbon on a White Horse* (1987; originally published in 1950). For example, in the autobiography, Yezierska hides key milestones in her life, such as a failed marriage and becoming a mother to a daughter. Moreover, it can be argued that literature, with its emphasis on emotions rather than actions, is superior to nonfiction if one wants to become truly immersed in the thoughts of people from distant times (Kidd and Castano 2013). This is usually a new concept for the students and opens an initial discussion of how historians draw on all sorts of evidence when interpreting bygone cultures and attitudes.

While students at Georgia Gwinnett College hail from a myriad of countries, ethnicities, and religions, none thus far share Yezierska's roots in Eastern European Jewry. In addition, few have ever had a close friend or acquaintance who is Jewish. Indeed, this material is so exotic that typically only the children of expatriates from the former Soviet Union will be able to pinpoint Poland on a map. However, I am a practicing Jew whose grandparents made a journey similar to the people portrayed in *Bread Givers*. When I reveal this personal information by showing how my own grandfather's voyage to the United States paralleled Yezierska's rail and ship voyage, the material in the book suddenly becomes less abstract. I can also vouch for the authenticity of the sentiments expressed by the author.

Knowledge about my background opens a preliminary discussion of how claiming a certain religious or ethnic identity can have varying influence on one's destiny. For example, although one may claim Eastern European Jewish roots, in other ways, he or she might have more in common with non-Jews from suburban Atlanta. Having the students learn about my ethnicity provides a welcome avenue for intimacy between me and the students.

From this point on in the course, a good number will begin sharing details of their own roots with the instructor and their classmates. These encounters happen inside and outside the classroom. They carry over to future semesters, in essence enriching the classroom experience for all as they gain firsthand experience of persons with diverse backgrounds that may not have been unmasked otherwise.

Yezierska, nicknamed the "Sweatshop Cinderella" because of her brief stint in Hollywood after a youth spent toiling in urban garment factories, is a fascinating figure to introduce to students. In her works, she is an astute critic of her plight of "wandering between worlds." The writer's feistiness made her unsuited to conform to the strict Orthodox Jewish religious customs in which she was raised, yet she found herself alienated by America's internal cultural tensions.

She was not alone among first-generation Americans in feeling estranged, but her feminist attitudes made her even more of an outsider in the cultural milieu of the early twentieth century. Because Yezierska was so modern in her outlook toward gender roles, today's students, whether they are male or female, feel a certain affinity with her perspective.

Born around 1880, Yezierska was the youngest of nine children raised in a "straw thatched hut" in a shtetl (a village) near Warsaw. She fondly recalled aspects of life back in Poland, such as the security of her close-knit family and the Jewish rituals that structured daily existence. However, like others who lived in the Pale of Settlement, marginal parts of the Russian Empire set aside for Jews, they were threatened by pogroms (Daniels 2002). Jewish fathers and sons feared being drafted into the military and "forced to drink vodka with the drunken *mouzhiks* (peasants), eat pig, and shoot [their own] people" (Dearborn 1988).

As was the case for many immigrant families at the turn of the century, a male relative was the first to leave home. Once Yezierska's older brother was settled, he brought over the rest of the family to live on the Lower East Side of Manhattan. The family settled on Hester Street, the epicenter of what was the most densely populated neighborhood in the world, with seven hundred people per square acre (Foner 2011).

Fortunately, Thomas Edison Company films make it possible to show students exactly what it looked like to arrive at Ellis Island and make one's way in that neighborhood. There is wonderful footage from 1903 depicting scenes of Jewish and Italian immigrants as fishmongers and pushcart sellers.

The backdrops for the action in the street are storefronts with Yiddish signage and dingy tenements like the one that provides the setting for high drama in Yezierska's books (Thomas A. Edison, Inc. 1903).

To give students a taste of the extinct world of the shtetl, they view a clip from the 1922 feature film *Hungry Hearts* (Hopper 1922). This silent picture was based on Yezierska's 1920 novel of the same title (Yezierska 2012). It was "discovered" by producer and fellow émigré Samuel Goldwyn, born Shmuel Gelbfisz, in Warsaw in 1879. Goldwyn paid Yezierska an exorbitant sum of money to relocate to Hollywood for her first trip outside New York so that she could vouch for the realism of the movie's sets and costumes. The producer also contracted the novelist to write what he hoped would be more hits for his fledgling studio. Such a Hollywood ending never materialized for Yezierska. She felt totally adrift amid the "tall Hawaiian pines of Beverly Hills." Unable to overcome her angst at being away from the gritty community that inspired her fiction and questioning her "position with those who grew rich at the expense of the poor," she suffered from writer's block and never earned her $100,000 fee (Yezierska 1987). After returning to the Lower East Side, her productivity returned, but her fame waned in the coming years. She died in obscurity in 1970.

The opening scene of Goldwyn Pictures' *Hungry Hearts* depicts a shabby village inhabited by women hard at work tending to barnyard animals. Then the action shifts to a mother baking ceremonial Jewish challah while a white-bearded father dressed in a long black cloak oversees a group of unruly young children learning how to read the sacred Torah. The stark contrast between men's and women's activities in the film is the perfect setup for a brief discussion of the gender and religious issues that will be dealt with in a discussion of *Bread Givers*.

In *Bread Givers*, the dramatic tension is fiercest between the sexes. The sharpest conflict occurs because father Reb Smolinsky spends his days studying Jewish texts as he had done before moving to the United States. The women—the mother and her four young daughters—must engage in factory work to put bread on the table, both literally and figuratively. Meanwhile, Reb insists on arranging marriages through a matchmaker, as was the practice in Poland. The girls, however, expect to adopt the modern American custom of selecting their own husbands. Sarah, the rebellious youngest daughter, goes one step further than her sisters, who are content with becoming dutiful wives and mothers as a means of escaping their poverty. "I must first make myself for a person," she declares. For Sarah, this means attending college and becoming a schoolteacher. But Reb attempts to thwart her aspirations, claiming that she is defying God's will (Yezierska 1975). Also working against Sarah's goal of self-sufficiency are America's own patriarchal conventions and class biases. In the early twentieth century, the assumption was that education should not stand in the way of marriage and homemaking as a primary female occupation.

Fortunately, students who typically complain about reading an entire book find Yezierska's novel downright entertaining and have no trouble finishing in a short time. Because students do not have to grapple with the prose—except for the occasional Yiddish expression—they can delve straightforwardly into the gender, religious, cultural, and class conflicts that are revealed in the characters' interactions.

"DON'T JUDGE ANY MAN UNTIL YOU HAVE WALKED TWO MOONS IN HIS MOCCASINS"

When students arrive in class on the day that roles from *Bread Givers* are assigned, this proverb, attributed to Native Americans, greets them on the white board in the front of the classroom. The students are asked to consider what the saying means, and within minutes they are providing a definition of *empathy* that is employed in the study of turn-of-the-century immigrants. After they learn which characters they will embody, those with laptops take a peek at summaries of the book. Students who remember to bring their copies of the novel to class flip through the pages to find where their names are used. *Bread Givers* works well for this exercise because it has fifteen characters, so just a few students will share a role. The women in the class portray one of the daughters, their mother, or their stepmother. Most of the men act as husbands or jilted suitors.

For students who have difficulty with reading comprehension, being assigned a specific character to follow makes it easier for them to navigate the entire book. The instructor asks them to read with pen in hand and tells them to underline and take notes on the events in which their character is involved. This teaches them to be discriminating researchers as they assemble qualitative evidence from the text that they will use later to arrive at a plausible interpretation.

The writing assignment is far from a typical history paper. Students are required to imagine that the father in *Bread Givers*, Reb (no one is assigned this role), has died and that their assigned characters are asked to speak at his funeral. The task is to write a 750-word eulogy for Reb in the first person from their character's perspective, not their personal points of view.

For the next two weeks, students in this course are seen around the campus reading a familiar red-and-green paperback. During this period, several students in every class will report that this is the first book they've read cover to cover in ages (or ever). A few will ask about the meaning of the Yiddish expressions or express rage at the irritating behavior displayed by Reb.

A quiz on basic plot elements and characters in the novel is part of the exercise. This ensures that students are keeping up with their reading. If they are reading diligently but missing out on key details, a poor grade will encourage them to reread or read more carefully before they compose their essays. Grades on these quizzes are usually the highest of any in the semester, which boosts enthusiasm and solidifies confidence in the reading instruction.

When this assignment was first tested, a mock funeral for Reb was held on the day the papers were due. Students were asked to read their eulogies aloud and then to discuss the salient issues. In the arrangement currently used, the instructor is a stage manager, assembling small discussion groups that function according to a few guidelines. Members of the groups each represent a different character in *Bread Givers*, and they elect a group leader to ensure that necessary tasks are completed. The exercise begins with each group member taking a turn reading his or her eulogy to their small group. This serves as an icebreaker because students are unlikely to know one another personally.

To make sure the subsequent discussion focuses on the issues of identity that arise from the study of immigration, students are provided with a printed chart that asks them to note how well each character adapted to American life and the factors (gender, age, religious beliefs) that influence the transition, whether they benefitted personally from the move from Europe or not, and their understanding of Reb.

The small groups work together for an entire class session to collect this information. When the class returns for the next session, each group reports its findings to the whole class. Students are asked to clarify their responses by "getting into character." Some students are uncomfortable playing "pretend," but others derive pleasure from adopting the boisterous language and Yiddish colloquialisms in the book. The atmosphere is lively when the more extroverted students are inspired to reenact some of the novel's vivid scenes.

The students who play the roles of the younger immigrant men in the novel add to the insights offered by Yezierska's tale when they offer that their characters' relative youth provides them with an advantage in securing the American Dream, which involves being a successful "bread giver." Young immigrant men's opportunities were more expansive than their elders and immigrant females because the United States prized the ambitions of young able-bodied men at the height of the industrial era. The students also explore why Sarah, the youngest daughter in the novel, is the lone Smolinsky daughter to rebel against their father's matchmaking.

The students who play the roles of the older daughters help the class to discern that age on arrival has a great deal to do with the situation in which the immigrant girls find themselves. The older the daughters are, the less chance they have to attend school and the greater allegiance they hold toward traditional marriage customs. For example, the eldest daughter, who immigrates as an adult, is the first to succumb to her father's choice of a groom, a widowed fishmonger. Although the match is a loveless one, it promises security to the daughter, who has toiled in sweatshops to support her family.

When the discussion ends, the insights are distinctly different than what one would derive from reading about immigrants in a textbook. By making a good-faith effort to adopt an insider perspective, there is no dwelling on the immigrants as burdens on their adopted homeland. Rather, students came to understand the reverse: how the pressure to adapt created unanticipated challenges and opportunities for the newcomers.

CONCLUSION

The essays for this exercise are typically better writing samples than others assigned in introductory history courses. Most students apparently relish being freed from the perfunctory five-paragraph expository formula and find that they are able to maintain the unique voice of their immigrant roles. However, the eulogy format, which requires the writer/speaker to deliver a coherent statement about another's character, provides enough structure for a solid piece of writing.

A handful of students derive creative inspiration from the role-playing, going beyond the basic requirements. In one instance, a student wrote a poem to reflect the pathos of her assigned female role, the eldest daughter, who is called Bessie the "burden bearer" because she sacrifices all youthful amusements to work on behalf of the family.

Other signs that this is a successful exercise are the outside-of-class conversations that are prompted by students. One student decided to investigate her Italian American roots and asked how to trace them. An Eritrean-born student, "Rahel," shared the similarities and differences she found between Yezierska's perspective and her own as a recent immigrant. She was struck that the America immigrants encountered a century ago and the one she entered twenty years ago reflected a "world for young people." If "Rahel's" African parents moved to the United States, then they would be as loyal to their Old World customs as the elders in *Bread Givers*, she remarked. "Rahel" also mentioned how changing gender mores have affected female migrants' adaption to life in the United States. This student, like the central character in *Bread Givers*, views attainment of higher education as her path to independence and satisfying the American dream. But "Rahel's" journey that will culminate in becoming a nurse has been less fraught because her parents support her ambitions, and the barriers blocking women's entrance to a profession have fallen.

Another student, "Becca," who was a born and raised in Georgia, subsequently asked for help with a project she was doing for her teacher education class. The class demanded that students explore the background of someone of a different ethnicity from their own to prepare for teaching elementary school pupils of varied nationalities. "Becca" wanted to delve more deeply into Yezierska's background than I and my students did in the survey course and learn more about Judaism because this was her first exposure to the religion. At the end of the semester, she produced a slideshow on the value of teaching Yezierska in a multiethnic classroom. One portion of the project indicated that "Becca" had made sense of the intersectional approach that was applied in the role-playing exercise. She had composed a slide showing that Yezierska's struggles as a new American were complicated by multiple identities: female, Jewish, and poor. Merely being immigrant did not reveal the nature of her adaptation to a new culture. Although this exercise has been repeated at least half a dozen times, the positive feedback from students about how much they enjoy reading and discussing the book has delayed making a change in how I teach it.

Chapter Eleven

Yellow Star of Courage

Teaching and Learning about the Holocaust

Louis Schmier

This chapter centers around student experiences in a two-hour general core course on the Nazi Holocaust that was taught at Valdosta State University (VSU), a large public school in Georgia with more than 9,700 students, between fall 2006 and fall 2012.[1]

Nazi Holocaust: two words for which, as Elie Wiesel said, there are no words. Two words that are so surreal that they are, as one writer describes, the "stuff of apocalyptic fiction" (Rapold 2013). But, they were real. So, the problem was how to make those two words real to the students—that is, how to convert the statistics of upward of twelve million human deaths by a deliberate government policy of extermination into a comparable number of human tragedies and convey the reality of the horrors of human tragedy inflicted by the inhumanity of it all. How to prevent a "defleshing" of these complicated and complex people into inanimate and spiritless stick figures with charts, statistics, and simplistic sweeping generalities; or sucking the life out of them with a list of names, places, numbers, and dates; or deperson-alizing them with lectures on sweeping -isms, theories, philosophies, theologies, generalities, and stereotypes. How to help them experience it and to see the relevance of it all to their individual lives. How to do all this without distracting the students with concerns of doing assignments, taking tests, and getting a course grade.

Yes, though there were no lectures or tests but contracted A's with the students as long as they did everything asked of them, every day the students would read survivor memoirs, watch testimonial films both in and out of class, listen to invited survivors and liberators of the camps, and submit daily answers to reflective questions. As one student observed, the class required "work, work, work, work, work."

There was, however, a problem. All the assignments were "spectator work." While the students were engaged in watching work, listening work, writing work, reading work, they were not experiencing the hardest of the works, engaged emotional work. Remember, the ultimate purpose of the course was to make it relevant and meaningful by having the Holocaust's nightmarish issues spill into their daily lives, touch their psyches, and test their values. As a solution to this problem, on the third day of class, for reference, the students received what was called a "Holocaust Ladder of Hate," the bottom rung of which was "stereotype." On the ascending rungs, in increasingly larger font, was "ridicule," "prejudice," "scapegoating," "discrimination," "expropriation," "ghettoization," and "extermination."

What the students did not know was that there were "secret" plans for them to experience the first three rungs, let them both infer how the other rungs would evolve and find their way to relating it to being targets of prejudice themselves as women, Asian, Spanish American, black, jocks, geeks, Greeks, blonds, full-sized, Catholic, Mormon, left-handed, and so on.

The Ladder of Hate was the scaffold of a design to initiate a focus on humanity in an otherwise inhuman situation. That design would piece together a picture that would offer an insight on a very individual human level that would focus on the dehumanization process of destruction, for this is what the intent of the course was: to somehow individualize and personalize an otherwise impersonal process and to make *Holocaust* a verb in the sense that students would have an understanding of the action involved. That design would cultivate in the students' endless, daily experiences that would stretch their hearts and minds, experiences that could be subtle as a gentle breeze or powerful as a gust of wind. That design was a daring, risky, administratively unpopular semester-long, daily assignment. The students would become Jews!

The syllabus read:

The Star

Now this is not an easy assignment. Maybe the hardest and most demanding of your college experience. But, to have you have that emotional experience, an experience anything near what it meant to be an isolated, expropriated, disenfranchised, persecuted member of the Jewish community, I can't throw you into a concentration camp, starve you, work you to death, or summarily kill you. But, I am requiring that you "bear witness," that you wear, pinned on the left side of your chest, on the outside of anything you wear, uncovered, unhidden, rain and shine, night and day, a visible a 4"×4" yellow, six-pointed Jewish star, in the middle of which is printed the word *Jew*. For the entire semester, you will wear this star wherever and with whomever—wherever and with whomever—you go *seven days a week, on and off campus: campus functions, class, church, home, socializing, etc., etc.* You will separately journal each day, in as much detail as possible, how people reacted to you, how you responded to them, and reflect on how you felt. The only exception to this requirement is if you work and your employer refuses to let you wear the star.

In their first journals, the responses were as varied as the students. There was mostly "What the hell is this?" surprise, "Is this guy serious?" confusion, "I can't do this" horror, "I'm not sure I can do this" hesitation, "I'm so shy" anxiety, "I don't want people to point at me for being different" fear. There were a very few "This is going to be interesting" excitement and a "It's going to tell me what I'm made of" challenge.

These extensive entries are how one student described that first day of class and the two that followed:

Day 1

We were each given a yellow Star of David with JEW written on it, and he told us we were to wear it every single day, everywhere we went. I looked at it. Then, I looked at him. I kept thinking this man is crazy. I'm not wearing this thing and that none of my classmates were going to do it. I kept thinking I was going to look stupid and that I would get stares and people would question me. He then went on to say that it was all a test to see if we could hold out and so we would be able to experience one hardship from the Holocaust. That's when my eyes really opened up. From that moment I decided I was going to follow through with this assignment because it would be such an eye opener for me. As I left the classroom it didn't take long for the stares and the comments to arise. It felt so weird just trying to exit the building. So many people in the hallway and many eyes were on my fellow classmates and I [*sic*]. I could hear people making snide comments under their breath and laughing. I finally got out of the building and ran into one of my friends. The first thing she noticed beside my new hair cut was this huge yellow star on my shirt. She began to laugh and was like why are you wearing that [*sic*]. I told her it was for class and how the assignment was to wear it every day wherever we go. The first thing she said was that it was stupid and that she wouldn't wear it and how she would just take it off. She even went on to say that she had wanted to actually sign up for the class, but that she was glad that she didn't because she wouldn't wear this, in her words, "stupid thing." That's when I realized that this is exactly the point that the professor is trying to get across. Just how blind people are about the past and how we are being ostracized for something so minute? She decided that she was going to eat lunch with me and so we went to Moe's. I had completely forgotten about the "SOD" [Star of David], but it didn't take long because as I sat down after getting my food the stares and comments were back. I looked around and eyes were on me again. I kept thinking this is getting ridiculous and I was so ready to get out of there. I thought well I have a class next so no one will be paying attention to me. . . . AGAIN I was wrong. I walked into this 150+ classroom and took my seat. The professor had us get up and introduce us to our classmates who were sitting on our row. My group, after getting to know me, asked why I was wearing the

SOD. I had to once again explain. I was really starting to get annoyed and wanted to take it off because I'm not a person who's really big on drawing attention to myself, but it looks like I'm now taking center stage. This journal entry is starting to look like a paper, but so much has already happened because of my wearing the SOD, and it's only the first day! I went to the bookstore and the bus stop, two places that were really busy, and I continued to get stares. I finally made it home, and my roommate opened the door for me. The first thing she did was give me this weird look, and her boyfriend made this really dumb joke; he said I was "racist" for wearing it. Even though it was him joking, it was still ignorant to say something like that. Well I've made it home, and I'm sitting here typing all of my day. I don't know if I'm going to be able to make it, but I'm going to stick to it and stay strong.

Day 2

I thought yesterday was going to be rough; today was even crazier. I had to journey all over VSU today because I had to get some things situated for the school year. I woke up and remembered that I had to wear my star because that was a requirement of the class, and I wanted to really get the experience. Once I got to the bus stop, I completely forgot about it. I had my headphones in, so I was more focused on my music. I went to my first class, and obviously, I couldn't play music. I did not realize that the class was a 150+ and I was already like two minutes late. I entered the classroom and as always when someone is late, everyone draws attention to the late comer. I looked all around the classroom and couldn't find a seat. I eyed an empty seat in the front and hurried on down. I could just feel all eyes being on me although the teacher was going over her syllabus. A technician was there to tell us about a program that we would be using for the class and she just continued to stare at me throughout her entire discussion.

After that class I had another soon after which was in Jennett Hall. I waited outside of the classroom alongside other classmates. It didn't take long for someone to take notice of the star. A girl tapped me on the shoulder and said that she saw me in her class yesterday, but as she was talking to me she had this puzzled look on her face. She finally had the confidence to ask me what the purpose of me wearing the star was. I told her that it was a class assignment and the premise behind it. Before she even noticed the star she wanted to sit by me in class and even become study buddies hopefully. But when we entered the classroom she sat five seats down from me. It didn't really affect me though.

I left that class and was heading to the crosswalk. Another girl was in front of me and asked me something (which I do not remember), then she asked what the star was for. So I found myself explaining the premise behind the star again. I was really getting tired of telling people. I didn't have my next class until a little later so I decided to check out the new Chick fil A [*sic*] in the Student Union. I met up with some friends that already knew about the assignment, but they made jokes as I made it over to them. One of my male friends made the joke that "your dad's a pastor. He would be ashamed." I thought to myself "Really, are you serious right now? What in the world does that have to do with anything?" I just made conversation with them and decided to go get some lunch. I went into the Student Union and there were SO MANY PEO-PLE in there! People were staring from every direction, but I didn't care. I think that it isn't really affecting me as much. I really do like journaling about what I have to deal with because it is making it easier to be proud to wear the sticker and actually have people wondering what the purpose is. I think that it helps remind people of the Holocaust, but they don't really take into consider-ation that people are singled out and hated on every day because of the color of their skin, their sexual orientation (if that's even the word for it), their religious views, and the list goes on.

As of right now I believe that more people should take this class so they get the experience. This is something I think everyone should try.

So many people already knew why I was wearing the star and would ask "You must be in Schmier's class." Later in the day I had an errand to run where I needed to go to the Education Building. As soon as I came in the door the front desk worker had a smile on her face, but the smile went away as soon as she saw the star. I soon told her it was for class. She told me that she figured and that whenever she sees people with the star she in her own words "give them a hard time." I'm just sitting here like how am I supposed to take this right now [*sic*]. But just said whatever and handled my business [*sic*]. I headed back to my room and took a nap with my star on. I woke up and went downstairs to the store with my roommate and the cashier asked like everyone else who's so eagerly curious what was the star was for. I'm telling you I'm really getting tired of explaining the purpose. It feels like it's taking this week forever so I can only imagine how the rest of the semester is going to be. Anyways [*sic*] we went back into the building and were waiting on the eleva-tor. There was a girl on the elevator who I met last semester. The first thing she noticed (see the pattern here) was the star and asked me "Are you Jewish?" I laughed and said no and that it was a class assignment. A few minutes ago I got off the phone with my parents and told them about what all I've been going through during the last two days. I told them that I had to wear the star 24/7 and not to be surprised when I came home with it on and me wearing every-where we go. To my surprise that were really accepting and with the idea 100%. That made some of the worry go away and it helped me to realize that it was going to be a little bit easier wearing the star every day. I don't think it really phases me until someone has the courage to ask me the purpose of the star. I honestly forget that it is even there. . . .

Day 3

It has been one long day, let alone a long three days. I think today was the day that I actually had a revelation because as of right now I just feel so good about myself and the courage I had to stand up for something I strongly agree in. Aside from having to wear the star today I was able to confront my roommate about the jokes she is constantly making about black people. Every day she tells me some joke about "black people" or she will make a comment such as "you are so ghetto" or something similar. Today was the day that I had had enough.

Today in class we were given a paper that had the different things that build the ladder of hatred. I had people who were my friends point at me and joke around and scream "JEW" and just laugh and walk away. I could do nothing but just shake my head and continue walking.

When I came home later tonight my roommate had wondered where I had been because I was all dressed up. She asked me "Did you go to some backwards KKK meeting that is for Black People or is there a secret black society that no one knows about" and would simply laugh. It was one of those "I didn't mean anything by it" and the "I was only kidding" and "no big deal" jokes. Well, it is a big deal. I just went to my room and shut the door. It was then that I realized exactly what Prof. Schmier was talking about and why he handed us the ladder of hatred sheet. This same thing was happening to the Jews. They were becoming the joke which led to a stereotype, then prejudice, discrimination, scapegoat, expropriation, separation, and then finally extermination. It's like everything was just clicking for me now. It was all starting to make sense. I am now going through just a little bit of what the Jews had to go through because it all started just by someone making a joke. It has happened in the past for African Americans and for people to make comments or jokes just because of the color of someone's skin is just the bottom of the ladder.

I just decided that I couldn't take it any longer and I just had to let her know how I really felt. I've known her since last semester, but the jokes were starting to get worse and worse and they started to irritate me because I was not saying anything and she was getting too comfortable. I really told her how I felt and how it was even affecting my friends when they were around her. She told me that she was so used to it and didn't know that it was affecting me. She said that the reason that she was joking was because of the people she was around. That growing up this was something that was so common for her, but I told her that what she has to realize is that this is something that is wrong. She told me that she didn't want people to stop being her friend so she went along with them. I had to tell her that by her continuing to make jokes and comments it's really making her out to sound racist and that it isn't funny. She said that she didn't want people to think that she was and that the people who joked with her would think something was wrong. What she failed to realize is that her purpose is not to please people and that they were not the right group of friends to be hanging around. They see it as something that is not wrong and of course by hanging with them she believes that it is okay as well. When in reality she is being ignorant [*sic*]. I told her how just in three days this project was working and that it had become a real eye opener for me and not just in the aspect of my race or Jewish persecution, but with anything that makes a person or a group of people different. She realized that she was put in the same situation freshman year when she had people who she thought were her friends gang up on her because she was not sure about her religion. By me really explaining the premise of the assignment, what I've been going through the past few days, and having to deal with her jokes, she really understood where I was coming from and we had a heart to heart moment. Which felt really good to me. I just feel like the star is making me stronger and it's only been three days.

She was not alone. All the students were experiencing a host of "I didn't mean anything by that" jokes, "It isn't a big deal" teasing, "I was only kidding" laughter, and "Get over it." And, over the weeks they were making this personal experience a deeply, intensely relevant connection to their own lives. For example:

> The Whispers. Stares. Rudeness, glares, ridicule, jokes. Comments. Questions. Disapproving facial expressions. It's creepy what's behind those smiles.

> What changed my perspective on the class was when you passed out the stars, and asked us to experience only a fraction of the prejudice the Jewish people experienced. I guess that in the end, I want this experience to be life changing and make me a better person that is not afraid to stand up for what is right despite the social stigma.

> I immediately felt self-conscious. All I could think about was "Is everyone looking at me? What are they thinking?" I got a few looks on campus today, but as I walked the halls I literally felt like everyone was staring at me, whether they really were or not. And of course this wearing the star thing got me thinking.

> I went back to my dorm, looked in the mirror, I wondered how this star would affect my social life. "So, you going to drop this course?" No, I said to myself. Ordinarily, I would have, but not this time. I don't know why. Maybe it was time.

> I didn't go anywhere again today because i [*sic*] didn't have my car for the longest time. However, I did go to an interview with my star. The man was interested in asking me why I wore the star and what did it represent to me. During my interview (in the middle of all the "why would you be good for this job") the manager said "If you don't mind me asking, what is the reason you wear this star today?" I then explained the idea that you had and the manager explained that it was really kind of a brave thing to be doing due to the fact that I showed up to an interview with it. The good thing about wearing the star is that most of my interview was questions about it and why I was wearing it, and not much of them asking me about the job. And, the manager said that it showed dedication and commitment. I got hired on the spot because of it.

> People look at me weird, and stare.

> Was walking from the bookstore and somebody actually yell [*sic*] "you dirty Jew" at me.

> This guy even walked up to me and laughed at me like I was crazy,

> We went to a viewing of a family member that died. Most people angrily looked at me.

When I completed my exam I walked to my professor [*sic*] desk and turned it in. As I was leaving he sarcastically said, "So you are Jewish today?"

When I walked out of class with my star on I immediately felt self-conscious. I have never been the type of person who likes a lot of attention and people staring at me. I am having a really hard time getting used to people staring at me. I tried to ignore it but I caught myself putting my hair over the star or rushing what I was doing to get out of the store as fast as I could. I honestly didn't realize how hard it was going to be to wear the star and feel like such an outcast. I'm already seeing the changes in people around me towards me.

I'm still struggling to stop my friends from joking about the star. I had an entire room of people laughing at me . . . damn it. This is hard! I realize that's the point. The fact that what the Jewish population went though is exponentially worse than what you've asked us to do. I still find myself struggling. . . . Hopefully by the end of this semester, I'll have the nerve to tell people that what they are saying is inappropriate and they should stop.

So today as I was wearing my star a friend approached me in what I assume was in a joking manner said "You can't be a Jew, you don't have their nose. . . . " Though I know they were joking it still kind of hit a sensitive spot for me because not only was it uncalled for, but it also was a stereotype that people use for others in the Jewish community.

My college life has changed dramatically in just three days.

This is going to make a difference in my life. I feel it. I guess that in the end, I want this experience to be life changing and make me a better person that is not afraid to stand up for what is right. I don't want to be a by-stander anymore.

Wearing this star that says "Jew" is like me, an African-American, wearing a sign that says "nigga." I am beginning to feel a sensation of a self-compelling personal crusade to go right my past myself and to begin a new chapter of my life.

I have finally become one with the STAR. The STAR is becoming my new identity for myself. It's taken a few weeks, tough weeks, but it has burned its way into my heart. It's done with a lot of the others [*sic*].

Today walking across the street to the student union, a stopped car pulled up just as soon as I stepped in front of her car. I looked up out of shock. The driver was staring at me with a disgusted look, pointed at my star, laughed, and ended with flicking me off.

While wearing it, every time I had a thought about someone else that would've been prejudice I stopped and thought about it and tried to remember that everyone is human. Everyone has a soul and feelings. I also noted the people around me and their prejudice comments. I'm trying to focus on that now in the beginning so I can avoid saying them.

The star helps remind me about my own thoughts of others. Even just being in the class has made me begin to notice how stereotypical thoughts form. People are surrounded by them. We grow up with them. We learn them from our parents and friends and it becomes a natural habit to say things like Asians are such bad drivers . . . which is something I did think when I nearly witness [*sic*] someone get hit by a car driven by someone Asian. Makes me wonder which came first . . . the stereotype or the behavior. When I have thoughts like that but harsher, I don't feel very good about myself. Sometimes they come out of anger (these are the harsher ones) and other times they are just simple things that everyone says.

Where does it end? If we're not careful we'll climb that "ladder of hatred" and wind up as perpetrators in a holocaust.

People look, ask, and absolutely judge the Star when they see it. But, they stop seeing me.

I've noticed myself trying to hide the star when I'm in public. I don't want people to see it because I'm afraid they will look at me. I don't want to stand out, I want to blend in. I feel so vulnerable and alone.

When I walked out of class with my star on I immediately felt self-conscious. I have never been the type of person who likes a lot of attention and people staring at me.

Wore the star in Walmart. I could. I honestly didn't realize how hard it was going to be to wear the star and feel like such an outcast. I'm already seeing the changes in people around me.

Ridicule from some professors. Teachers look at me with a weird expression as if I was some wild animal. Even if I was just sitting in the classroom, I seemed to stick out. I felt like an unwelcome feeling in some of my classes.

One day, after about three weeks of wearing the star, a student wrote in her journal, "I can't do this alone and be alone. If only I had someone else with me I can stand the looks and words." At the same time, another bemoaned and wished, "My college life has changed dramatically in just three days. The teasing, the laughter, the ridicule, and no one coming to help me. People I have never seen before walk up to me and nastily call me 'Jew.' But, I don't know if I can do this much long alone." A third asked, "I wonder if anyone in the class is in the same situation as me. I'd feel better if we could share."

In response to these entries, a "Star Circle" was created, in which the students shared their experiences, feelings, and reactions. One of those three students wrote that night, "Knowing there were others in the same boat as me and had my back, gave so much courage to go on." Another wrote,

Today at star circle it really opened my eyes to how much the star has made a lot of us grow. I know it has made me grow because not only do I still stand up for myself but I am more aware of the way I refer to people. I use to describe a person to someone else by saying, "oh they are white, or oh they are black." And now I try to make sure that I not label them by their skin color. I am also very aware of the way my friends treat other people. When they try to judge someone before they know them then I step up and say would you want someone to do that to you or would you rather them judge you by the way you look? This star has had an impact on not only me but the people that are in my everyday life as well.

When at one "Star Circle" session one student tearfully related how she was accosted by a "heil Hitlering" foreign exchange student, the entire class decided to go with her to confront her ridiculer. "We have formed into a family that will stick together come what may," a student explained. "And that is something you cannot find in any regular class. We are all linked because of these yellow stars. They have burned their way into our hearts."

The "Star Circle," held about every three weeks or as necessary, was a watershed for a lot of the students:

"This light felt star was getting heavy, too heavy, very quickly. Knowing others are feeling the same during star circle makes it bearable."

"Walk with me if you want. Don't if you're afraid. 'Yeah, it's kinda weird to be walking with you now since you have that,' my friend said, 'but I do think it's for a good reason so I don't mind walking with you.'"

"I thought maybe you were joking. But, then when you explained why you were doing it, I got it. It's going to make us feel some of the emotions of those people who were persecuted. This class is like a ghetto where we're helping each other."

"Feel sad and haunted, but proud of myself for doing this."

"I am beginning to feel a sensation of a self-compelling personal crusade to right my past self and to begin a new chapter of my life."

"Yesterday I went to babysit wearing my star. I was scared. I explained it to the parents. They said it was a good way to understand the Holocaust and that I was a good role model for their children. I felt I was wearing a yellow star of courage."

"Went out to work today to pick up my check, and all my coworkers were exploding with questions. Why are you wearing that? How long do you have to wear that? Are you Jewish? Some were concerned they were offending me. Some thought I was brave to wear it. Others thought I was crazy, and that they'd be too scared to wear it. I liked the brave comment, because it does make me feel brave and inspirational."

"I feel extra happy to wear my star on this day. I feel as though God is looking down and is very proud of our class. We set out wanted [*sic*] to show and tell more about the Holocaust and we did."

"You're still doing that Jew thing? 'Yes,' I answered in a tone that surprised myself. Boy was he surprised. Thank you star circle!"

"The answer seems so small: hatred, good people doing nothing. No one comes to support me except my classmates. How can something so big happen because of something that seems so small as this star? It is then, the small actions every day that keeps the big things from happening. Small things, standing up for people, not allowing prejudices to walk past you with calling it for what it is. Not allowing yourself to separate people by any grouping. Those are the things that keep the big things from happening. On second thought, maybe it's not so small after all."

"This class by far has been my most challenging emotionally but the most rewarding as well. It is hard to put into words all this class has meant to me. I want to be someone who is willing to help someone if I can. I want to do the right things. I want to be a better person. These are some things the class taught me. I want all these things not just for me, but for my children. To make a difference you must first start with yourself."

"There is so much about this that simply [I] do not understand. I do not understand people getting on board with such a horrific thing. I don't understand the evilness that was the motivating force behind this atrocious act. I don't understand this blind belief in Hitler. . . . Nobody is supposed to understand this. No one should make sense of this; this should not be justified nor made a simple thing. Perhaps it is in our incapacity to understand this that we can become strong enough to not allow it to happen again."

"I began to wonder if the star is defining me or am I defining the star. I honestly am not sure, I think it is a little bit of both. It is helping me or should I say this class is helping define the person I want to be. Maybe though I am defining the star by no longer letting it be the butt of jokes or when it is I stand up for it. I do not let it be looked down on."

"Today as I was paying for gas the cashier looked/stared at my star for a long while as she was helping the person in front of me. My inner response to her was no longer embarrassment or self-consciousness but, I was proud to be wearing it."

"I have picked up the new nickname Jew from my friends. Maybe they're not as much my friends as I thought. No one is standing up for me. They're all by-standers. I know now how that feels."

"That star is my 'yellow badge of courage.' I will keep it my drawer long after this class is over."

"I was wearing the star to Waffle House. An elderly woman kept looking at me. She seemed upset. We both left at the same time. She turned to me and ask me why am I 'wearing such a thing.' She was angry. I explained how it was a class project to experience a little bit of what it was like being Jewish during the Holocaust and to remember those who died. She suddenly got tears in her eyes. 'I lost my family at Auschwitz. I was there. It is a good thing what you do. Thank you.' I was so surprised. As she got in the car, her husband turned to me, smiled and slightly nodded his head. Why didn't I talk more with her?

Can't tell you how I felt. It was like having my own private star circle. I'll never stop hearing her words. And to think I almost dropped this course the first day."

"When I went home that past weekend I walked in my house wearing my star. My parents already knew about the star that I was wearing for my class so they were not so surprised to see it when I walked in, my brother on the other hand did not share the same reaction. He seemed to be embarrassed about my star even though we were at home, and even though he did not have to wear it. He kept picking on me about it and making his little 'Jew come here' jokes. I decided not to give any attention to his jokes in hopes that he would stop, and soon enough he did. That Sunday I proceeded to get ready to go to church with my dad like I always do when I go home to visit. As we were starting to leave I went to my room to pin my star onto my dress with a lot of hesitation. I hesitated not because I did not want to wear it, but because I did not know how the members of my church were going to react to it. I knew that they were not going to be rude to me, or throw me out of the church but because I did not want to offend them. And because I knew that majority of the members there are very close-minded people. I finally decided to wear it and pinned it on my dress, and walked out to meet my dad. When I walked into the living room my brother was there and looked at me with the most appalled look I have ever seen. He asked, 'Are you seriously thinking you are going to wear that to my church?' I looked at him and said, 'Yes I am. I am going to wear this to OUR church.' He started to argue with me my about it until my dad stepped in and said we need to leave before we are late. I angrily walked away and left with my dad. When we arrived at the church I am not going to lie I was very nervous but I knew that I needed to go forth with it. I had gotten this far and knew that I could not just take it off at the doors. I walked into the church with my head held high and could already feel the stares. I knew they were not looking at the color of my dress, or my shoes, or anything else but that glowing yellow symbol. I had a few people hesitate as they walked by me, like they were going to question me about it but they kept walking. We had recently gotten a new preacher at my church and I had not gotten a chance to meet him yet, and my chance was going to come that day. As I followed my dad to our seat we ran into the preacher, and I saw his gaze fall onto my star. He did not pause, he asked me directly about my star. I began to explain the story behind the star and the class, and he seemed to be really moved by it. We began talking so much that he was late to start his sermon. He went up to the front and explained to the congregation that he had the opportunity to finally meet me at the back of the church and he was very moved by a school project that I was participating in. He said that he knew that majority of the people had already seen my star. And that he wanted me to come up for a short bit and explain to them the meaning behind it. So I went to the front and started to explain why I was wearing the star and the reactions that I was getting for it. After I started to explain my story to them, I could see their gazes soften because they could tell that I was not doing it for attention or to make a statement. They seemed to be very interested in knowing if anyone was rude or mean to me about it. After I was done talking to them about it my preacher started his sermon. He actually ended up redoing his sermon and made it revolve around the correct way we should treat people, no matter their race, religion, or other preferences. It was a very moving day for me. When I returned home after church my brother was there waiting to continue our unfinished conversation. He started into me again about how I was being disrespectful. Right when I was about to start yelling at him my dad stepped in and told my brother that he needed to shut up and listen to my story. He said, 'If you would just listen to your sister you would realize how much strength it takes for someone to actually do this task and succeed at it. Your sister is being more of a human being than you could ever hope to be because she is actually keeping an open mind to a new and somewhat scary experience.' After that my brother was quiet and allowed me to finish telling him about my experiences I was having with the star. As I told him some of my reactions I had gotten he seemed to be a little enraged. I told him he had no reason to be mad about the way some people were acting towards me because not even five minutes before he was acting the exact same way. The more I talked to him about it the more he wanted to know about it. So he finally came to the conclusion that he was going to make his own star and he was going to wear it like I was."

CONCLUSION

The students' final evaluations demonstrate the value of their experiences:

"This class is about me and everyone. It has merged my life in the class-room with my life outside the classroom. I wasn't just a reader, watcher, or writer. Set apart from my daily life. The star made me one of the actors in a play everywhere and at all times. It was inconvenient, uncomfortable, painful, weighty, and at times eerie, but oh how I needed it. This class has made me more aware of prejudice and discrimination in the world around me, and sad to say, in myself. But, maybe just as important I understand what the theme of this course meant, that for evil to exist good people need only to remain quiet. I see how so much in the class related to the whole outside the class-room, and I now see how such things can happen—and can be pre-vented."

"At first it was difficult to put on that first day. Then, it was difficult to wear the star every day everywhere. Now, it's difficult to take off the star. I have changed. I came into this class just to get a quick and easy A. Now as I leave this class, I feel it is all hitting me. Bittersweet. Happy. Sad. Thankful. Difficult. Uncomfortable. Amazement. Sa-cred. . . . so many words could be said to describe its meaning. We must make sure not to be seduced by the evil of this world, but instead stay firm in what we believe and why we believe it. I can see all of these things playing out in my mind, and it is awful. I can see the woman begging for her life, begging for mercy. I can see the sardine packing and the innocent people being shot with a blank look of fear and confusion in their eyes. The pictures were terrible; women trying to remain decent, rushing to their deaths, haughty men standing high above the mass graves yelling orders, to hurry along as to not slow down the "process." Yes, we must be individual enough not to be seduced by such wickedness. Whether or not I wear it, I don't think I will ever forget it. Now though because of this class I do, this class has bettered me to become a better person. I take up for people now more than I would normally. I am not the girl laughing with her group of friends. I am the one yelling at them for being rude. I am so happy with the person this class has turned me into being, it will be a most bittersweet end to my semester. Now, when I see someone, I think before I speak, I think before I act, and I never judge. I am not the same person I was when I started this class."

"I have gained such self-esteem. I feel like I can hold my head high and conquer anything life throws at me. Wearing that star has made me proud to be myself. I have always been afraid of what people think about me. My first thought is always what will everyone think. I should not be afraid of who I am. With the help of this class and wearing that star I am now not afraid and worried about what others think about me. This class has changed my entire outlook on life and more importantly on myself."

"For my last reaction I would like to talk about the most powerful reac-tion to my star—my own. It has been hard to where [*sic*] it in some public places, but most of all it has been hard to be consistently re-minded of the Holocaust. I find myself in public areas wondering what it would be like to be forced to leave, or if I see a police what it would have been like to worry that he will see my star and harass me because of it. People have noticed, asked questions, given looks, and made remarks, but my own reaction was one of grief and heartache for those who wore this star in a different time, they will never be forgotten. I will never forget."

"This class has led me to think twice about making ethnic and racial jokes; it has forced me to examine my own prejudices. It has taught me that if the world is to change, that change has to start with me. I became bolder and stronger within myself. I have become more conscious of my thoughts and the words I speak. I am no longer a bystander."

"I came to this class with an idea and am leaving it with an ideal."

"With everything I saw and experienced, I'm leaving this class feeling I've inherited a memory."

"It is amazing how one perspective course can make you, me, have a whole new perspective on life."

"Dr. Schmier told about a Jewish teenager, trapped in the Warsaw Ghetto, who wrote to a relative. He asked 'Who will remember I had once lived?' I guess I can answer that. I will."

That's all a teacher could ever hope to achieve.

NOTE

1. "General core" means that certain courses are required for all students.

Chapter Twelve

"Postcard from Auschwitz?"

Chronicling the Challenges of a Holocaust Study Abroad Program

Natalie Bormann and Veronica Czastkiewicz

In this chapter, a series of encounters, collected during a Holocaust study abroad program, provide the context for thinking through the challenges of Holocaust education at sites of trauma. It does so by synthesizing field notes from the program with existing scholarly debates on the subject matter. Two questions guide the writing here: First, how can one bring the often-traumatic experience of visiting sites of trauma into the fold of learning about the events at those very sites? Second, is there a conflict between the ethical imperative to remember the catastrophic past and the impetus to find ways to teach about it? In addressing these questions, we explore the themes of Holocaust travel as "death tourism" as well as the concept of students being "up against trauma."

The chapter does by no means intend to provide a roadmap for successful Holocaust study abroad programs—and it cannot do so. Nonetheless, in its concluding remarks, suggestions are made on how to alter some of the features of Holocaust education at sites of trauma.

NOTES ABOUT THE PROGRAM

Every summer, twenty-five undergraduate students from across campus at a private university on the U.S. East Coast embark on a Holocaust study abroad program to Germany and Poland. This program spans five weeks and takes students to five cities that are deemed central to the history of the rise of National Socialism and the Holocaust (Munich, Nuremberg, Berlin, Warsaw, and Krakow). The group visits three concentration camps (Dachau, Sachsenhausen, and Ravensbrueck) and stays overnight adjacent to the death camp of Auschwitz (in the town of Oświęcim). Other activities include participation in seminars, lectures, and workshops; visits to museums, documentation centers, and memorial sites; and meetings with survivors.

The program is based on two interrelated courses with four credit points each. A political science course teaches the history and politics of the Holocaust. In this context, students are prompted to think through the political ideology of National Socialism, fascism, and totalitarianism; the role of the nation-state and state violence; propaganda; roles and identities of victims, perpetrators, and beneficiaries; and the power of resistance and compliance.

The other course is located in international affairs and provides a more interpretative framework geared toward helping students to engage critically with the *representations* of the Holocaust. Here, the group probes debates on "museum politics" and genocide memory, the role of preservation and aesthetization of sites of trauma, and the overall significance of an always-shifting memorial landscape.

As is to be expected, such a journey presents itself with many challenges. These challenges are diverse in nature and are reflected to some extent in the literature on group and class excursions to sites of trauma (Blum 2004; Cowan and Maitles 2011; Schechter and Salomon 2005). Although there are not many significant scholarly contributions on extended Holocaust travel programs, three main categories of encounters stand out (Gray 2014).

There are practical issues (for instance, the often physical and emotional demands on the students), followed by pedagogical and academic ones (for instance, broader questions regarding the impact and purpose of on-site education). Finally, it is the ethical challenges that the program bears (for instance, the recurring debates on dark tourism or the [ab]use of social media at death camps). What follows is a brief journey through some features of these categories.

THE PREMISE: HOLOCAUST TRAVEL AS AFFECTIVE LEARNING

What do Auschwitz and visits to other sites of mass atrocity ultimately teach the learners? There are obvious answers to this question; the literature is quick to confirm that there seem to be "enhanced opportunities by the learner" by actually "living through" events at sites where history occurred (Clyde, Walker, and Floyd 2005). Teaching as "living through" speaks most fundamentally about the experience of the physical structures—the built environment, geography, and ruins—which is said to augment other existing forms of methodology and analysis, namely narrative history or visual representations (Trigg 2009).

Being at the actual ground where events took place can help in envisaging the depth and (scale of) the event. With that comes specific sensory features that accompany space—smells, sounds, images (Kranz 2013; S. Smith 2007). Accounts of student experiences at sites during this Holocaust study abroad program seem to support this. Students are very perceptive to the reality of the very large area of Auschwitz-Birkenau, for instance, which helps them to "imagine the scale" of the atrocities that they only knew from descriptions in documents, something that was hitherto only manifested in numbers (student comment). Similarly, a seminar at the Preservation Department at the Auschwitz Memorial Museum is an example of a sensory feature that affects students profoundly: The group is able to see, smell, and even touch a sample of the ninety thousand shoes—currently in the process of preservation—and that one normally sees on display behind the museum's glass wall. During one of the debrief sessions, students recalled feeling "deeply conscious" about the atrocities that the victims endured based not only on an astute sense of "reality" by "having been there [the space]" but also from the ability to investigate "close-up" the symbolic artifacts—"all of the shoes have a story," reflected one student.

The other major component of the experience of being there is rooted in the promise of specific cognitive and reflective outcomes. There are some studies that seek to investigate more astutely the exact relationship between students' involvement in experiential learning programs for Holocaust studies and specific skill sets—such as citizenship and leadership skills or social justice training (Blum 2004; Clyde, Walker, and Floyd 2005). Unfortunately, at this point in time, these studies are far from conclusive.

While it would appear that the study abroad infrastructure—the guts of the program—is becoming increasingly systematized and has certainly come a long way from its initial conception in 1938, the programs offered are in constant flux and often lack a rigorous structure of, for instance, follow-up procedures to reorient students upon return (Clyde 2005). This makes it challenging to deduct a more predictable set of data between the affective and cognitive experiences in student learning.

STUDY ABROAD AS OR IS DARK TOURISM?

Visits to sites of mass killing, battlefields, or cemeteries are often termed *dark tourism* (Ashworth and Hartmann 2005; Cole 2000; Lennon and Foley 2000; Sion 2014). There has been an increasing concern about such tourism; it captures fundamentally the fact that we *visit* places of suffering and atrocity to begin with, questioning our motivation for so doing. As Wulf Kansteiner puts succinctly, "we are engaging with violent pasts that we find disturbing, fascinating, and intellectually challenging" (2014, 403). To put it bluntly, we are "attracted to 'the dark side' of history" (Kansteiner 2014, 403). It comes as no surprise, then, to bear witness to the growth of "Holocaust tourism," with Holocaust museums and former camps playing the role of sites of "mass tourism" (Wollaston 2005, 63).

Tim Cole (2000, 110) speaks of "Auschwitz-land" and leaves no doubt as to his views on what he terms the "Holocaust heritage industry": "Auschwitz is to the Holocaust what Graceland is to Elvis," Cole insists (2000, 98). Another popular "joke" about the Holocaust tourism industry exclaims that "there's no business like Shoah business," calling to mind a dark mix of theatrical performance and the Hebrew word for catastrophe (Finkelstein 2000).

The critique of museums as "marketplaces" (Wollaston 2005) is widely shared even outside the academy; last year's Holocaust study abroad program was accompanied by the publication in a leading German newspaper that labeled Auschwitz the "Disneyland of death" (Broder 2014), a place where visitors can be "comfortably scared and shocked" (and entertained?). No doubt, the vast complex of Auschwitz-Birkenau represents perhaps one of the greatest and most compelling dilemmas of "dark tourism."

A Holocaust study abroad program needs to negotiate these critiques in two related ways. Initially, the *modalities* of Holocaust travel as an "activity" are under scrutiny. Isabel Wollaston distinguishes here between "primary" or "secondary" activity (2005, 65). For instance, visiting Holocaust sites is often incorporated in holiday package deals as a secondary activity by tour information bureaus—the morning at Auschwitz, the afternoon at Poland's famous Wieliczka salt mines. To what extent can a study abroad program avoid engaging in "secondary activity"? During a five-week journey, can the group really be expected not to engage in other, nonprogram-related activities—and should it be expected to do so? Is it OK to visit Dachau on one day and Neuschwanenstein Castle the next? And where to draw the line, especially once looking at sites other than museums? Each year, students visit the infamous Hofbraeuhaus in Munich in the morning to hear about Hitler's early political activities there before returning to the very same place in the evening for a celebration of Fourth of July. In other words, can one ever avoid the slippage into "secondary activities"?

The second point has to do with people's identity as tourists and its associated practices *at* the sites themselves: People dress leisurely, often ignorant that a site of trauma is in many cases also a site of commemoration; people have snacks and lunches only feet away from a place of mass killing; people take snapshots—"I was here"—just as we enter (and leave) through the *"Arbeit macht frei"* gate. Each year, the students make purchases at the camp museum shop; one can buy postcards, fridge magnets, and even a bracelet at Dachau. The group takes packed lunches to Dachau but decides to eat at the on-site restaurant at Auschwitz; "The prices there are reasonable," a student can be overheard uttering. After lunch, one can conveniently dispose of one's postcards at the post office adjacent to the restaurant, and money can be exchanged, too, if needed. The students in the group often lament the conflict they feel regarding their identity as tourists, something they argue is an inescapable role they are placed in due to the overall structure of the sites as tourist destinations. Would resisting purchasing fridge magnets at the Auschwitz memorial museum relieve the group from a feeling of being a tourist?

These tensions emerge, partially at least, from the extent to which it is not always clear what kind of "destinations" these sites in fact are. Wollaston writes that most Holocaust museums are "simultaneously tourist attractions and memorial sites" (2005, 66). This adds an additional layer of complication to the roles that most former sites see themselves fulfilling—that of a museum (historical representation), a memorial (commemorative or pilgrimage function), and an educational institution (a *Mahnmal*, a "warning").

Wollaston adds that while it may be possible to distinguish between memorial and museum, the distinction "often becomes blurred" (2005, 66). What in fact *are* the students expected to encounter, experience, and take away from these three realms? And do they happen all at the same time? The danger may well be that these three roles are in conflict with one another. A two-day visit to Auschwitz may illustrate this.

This study abroad program spends two days at Auschwitz (with an overnight stay at an adjacent hostel in the Polish town of Oświęcim); the purpose is twofold: first, to all together avoid reducing the visit to nothing more than exactly that—a visit—and to defy the attempt to teach about the Holocaust in a short space of time; and second, to focus on the educational experience that the site may offer. This includes a visit to Auschwitz and Auschwitz-Birkenau but also a set of educational programs that involves the aforementioned Preservation Department, the Archives, and the Press Office (to discuss the use of social media—"liking Auschwitz" on Facebook).

While these programs undoubtedly contribute to a more specific knowledge on the relevance of the site concerning the academic questions asked, students lamented a "fading of the emotional experience." One student talked about "feeling desensitized" after having walked through the gate that adorns Auschwitz more than a handful of times. Can we encourage cognitive and reflective skills without challenging the affective and commemorative ones?

"BEING AT" AND "UP AGAINST" TRAUMA

When we speak of the emotional affect as a learning component, it is easy to see how there can be a slippage into something that sounds less innocent— that of a deeper traumatic affect. Research shows that Holocaust education, especially when outside the classroom, produces emotive and powerful reactions and can even be extremely emotionally traumatic (Cowan and Maitles 2011; Gray 2014).

One of the students in the group—at Auschwitz—admitted that her therapist had cautioned her against visiting the death camp, for he was concerned about the impact it may have on his patient's state of mind/heart/soul, which seemed like a strong response to the existing research. It became clear that the said therapist discouraged this "opportunity" for feeling overburdened by the stress, anxiety, sadness, shame, and even responsibility that the student may experience. To argue that instances like these can unleash a challenge for educators would be an understatement. Initially, it is emotions of sadness and shame that are said to be the very experiences openly encouraged by museum curators and camp site pedagogues (Kranz 2013). The research on education at memorial sites proposes that, yes, some of the experiences can make students feel extremely uncomfortable and vulnerable; "these emotions, however, can be justified in educational terms and seem downright necessary for a productive encounter with the historical site and its past" (Wysok 2013, 66–67).

But the concept of vicarious trauma—the witnessing of pain and suffering of others—is important elsewhere. During the time of the most recent journey made with this program, the *New York Times* revisited the ongoing debate on the prevalence of anxiety in U.S. college students today, a phenomenon that is increasingly noticeable on college campuses nationwide (Hoffman 2015). Against the backdrop of studies that speak to the emotional impact of being exposed to sites of trauma, one must question seriously the framework of mixing Holocaust education with study abroad: How much do educators have to alter the components of the program so that it lessens the possibly "mounting pressure" on the students? Are we composing Holocaust "lite"? But how far can one go in creating as gentle an environment as possible without, perhaps, failing as an educator to convey the real depth of the horrors of the Holocaust?

In a contribution to the value and necessity of emotional "exposure" at former camp sites, Wiesław Wysok writes that teachers "should think *before* the visit about various practical things to do to help the pupils work out their emotions" (2013, 67, emphasis added). And so we do exactly that. The group participates in mandatory predeparture meetings; during one of those meetings, a trauma expert provides a workshop for the students on how to prepare for witnessing places of trauma. But does this suffice?

CONCLUSION: LESSONS LEARNED?

What these reflective encounters reveal is that the experience of a student "as tourist" during a Holocaust study abroad may be inescapable; the same may be said about the concept of being "up against" trauma located at sites of killing. The takeaway, then, lies in the extent to which one can perhaps amend this particular experience.

In this final section, two brief suggestions are made for improving the specific study abroad experience that is dissected here. The first is an invitation to rethink our role as educators; here, the suggestion is to take more seriously the concept of educators as curators (of an experience); that is to say, to think more carefully about the elements of a study abroad program within which the academic features are embedded (that which is on the margins).

The second suggestion sheds light onto the motives for visiting Holocaust sites—camps and museums—and emphasizes the role and significance of smaller, lesser-known sites. This may circumvent both the issue of appearing "out of place" as tourists and also the exposure to the often-traumatic experiences at death camps.

Educators as Curators

In his reflections on an educational trip to Auschwitz, Lawrence Blum (2004) draws an analogy between the role of museum guides and teachers or educators. The author remarks on the different scope of responsibility that separates guides from educators: the former's responsibility to the visiting students ends with the tour, so to speak; the latter's, however, extends beyond the visit to a site. Blum concludes that the relationship between guides and educators ought not to be overestimated, and in fact, perhaps the two roles are not comparable at all. To the contrary, there is indeed an interesting and useful comparison to be made here. While their level of responsibility may indeed vary, both guide and educator are, however, complicit in *curating* something akin to an experience for the students.

In the process of creating this study abroad program, we also found ourselves consciously "curating" how we wanted our students to experience this Holocaust travel. In other words, the activities outside and alongside the academic ones during Holocaust travel are just as central to the academic experience as, let's say, the accompanying syllabi. Thus, to modify the "tourist experience," this study abroad program has opted for a stronger emphasis on the academic component of study abroad. This means specifically, for example, that all museum and site visits are accompanied by a workshop or seminar on-site (and never "merely" a visit); students must write assignments on almost all their activities in order to avoid the role of simply "gazing at" sites without a particular framework for so doing; and there are less shared leisure activities as a group in order to maintain the integrity of the group as a study group.

No "Camp Site Hopping": Less Is Often More (Focus on Ravensbrueck)

In a conversation with the press officer at Auschwitz Memorial Museum about the recent progress in digital technology that allows one to "see" the site on one's technological device (a 360-degree tour, for instance), he nonetheless insists that "*nothing* can replace a visit [to Auschwitz]" (emphasis added). But coming away from three years of leading this study abroad program with all of its challenges for teaching about the Holocaust, we are not so sure.

What exactly does one "get" by visiting sites of trauma, and how many sites does one need to visit to ostensibly "get it"? As Stephen Smith recalls, experiencing a place's physical features and being brought close to the human suffering that occurred there "will not necessarily mean that the visitor knows a great deal more at the end of the visit" (2007, 273). What does the act of visiting and being there *do* beyond confirming that which we already think we know? In addition, to what extent can one avoid being a tourist when the structures at the very sites one visits preclude one from being anything but a tourist? As Tim Cole points out about the Auschwitz museum's entrance building that used to be the place where camp prisoners were initiated: Auschwitz has morphed from a place of prisoner initiation to tourist initiation (2000, 110). With that in mind, the program is emphasizing more the visit to other, lesser-known sites.

When visiting Ravensbrueck women's camp an hour north of Berlin, it is usually the first time students learn that such a camp in fact existed. It is not easy to reach the camp, and the group must walk through small neighborhoods of the adjacent village to get to the camp. There is no "famous gate" when one enters the camp, and you will find yourself in empty, open spaces, characterized by an absence of symbolic representations of violence. The camp is empty, devoid of tourists or long lines; conversations with guides and seminar leaders are personal and not rushed. The camp is calm and quiet and offers an unusual opportunity to feel not horror but emptiness, sadness, and melancholy. It is nothing like the thick symbolic representations that meet the group at the museum at Auschwitz.

It becomes clear very quickly that a museum and memorial site such as Ravensbrueck offers the spatial benefits of experiential education—it is a place where the Holocaust happened—minus the two themes problematized here: Students feel less part of mass tourism and also are less exposed to witnessing some of the raw horror of Nazi atrocity. Students comment on the "more personalized" approach at this smaller and less-recognized camp that allows them "to have more space and time" to engage in much more depth with the subject matter.

A set of questions discussed at the site illustrate the pedagogical depth; have women's experiences been different from that of men? Why do we rarely hear about female perpetrators? What is the rationale behind the political economy of former camp sites that has relegated Ravensbrueck to the margins of a Holocaust study program? What can we learn at a place that is devoid of visible traces of violence yet where violence inexorably occurred?

In exposing at least some of the concerns that were present during a Holocaust study abroad program, this chapter is keenly uneasy about the ways in which Holocaust travel may perhaps contribute to a self-indulgent education, at the center of which may be a student absorbed by vicarious experiences and cast into the role of trauma tourist. The conclusion is that the framework of study abroad for education about the Holocaust may at its core always already contribute to these effects; however, a more open engagement with the idea of educators as curators may allow teachers to choose more mindfully which activities may lessen both the experience as tourist and also that of trauma.

Chapter Thirteen

Speech, Diversity, and Higher Education

Balancing Civil Liberties and Freedom from Discrimination in Classrooms and Campus Life

Scott A. Boykin

To fulfill their mission, colleges and universities must provide an environment in which their students can learn. Federal laws and regulations prohibit the creation of a hostile educational environment based on a student's race, sex, national origin, religion, or disability, and state and local laws and regulations may protect students against a hostile educational environment based on these and other factors, such as a student's sexual orientation or gender identity. Colleges and universities have established speech policies to facilitate learning, comply with applicable laws, and avoid exposure to liability for failure to comply with such laws.

Faculty and administrators should be familiar with these speech policies and the laws and regulations those policies implement. Faculty often confront issues involving speech in the classroom, and administrators and faculty in their governance role should be informed about relevant legal authorities when framing campus speech policies. In recent years, there has been a wide-ranging public debate regarding such policies, which reflects concerns for both civil liberties and freedom from discrimination.

In addition, there has been much litigation prompted by both campus speech and speech policies, which has been based on the First Amendment as well as federal and state antidiscrimination laws. This chapter assesses the state of the law regarding discriminatory campus speech, analyzes the balancing act colleges and universities must perform when drafting speech policies, and offers guiding principles these institutions should consider when designing policies to balance freedom of expression with freedom from discrimination.

CONSTITUTIONAL LIMITATIONS

Several First Amendment issues often arise in disputes over campus speech. First, there are some types of speech that are not protected by the First Amendment. Campuses are free to regulate such speech provided the campus rules properly define and enforce speech falling into these categories. Second, there are formal characteristics that rules must have to satisfy First Amendment requirements for regulating speech. Third, governments and campuses may regulate the time, place, and manner of speech, and these kinds of regulation are particularly significant for campuses.

Further, there are issues involving the differences between private and public colleges and universities. While public institutions are certainly bound by the First Amendment, it is more difficult to hold private institutions accountable due to the state action requirement under constitutional law unless state governments require them to do so under state law, as, for example, California has done (Sanders 2006, 177 and n. 143). Private institutions are nonetheless bound by federal civil rights statutes, discussed later.

UNPROTECTED SPEECH

The following categories of speech are not protected by the First Amendment. As a result, they can be regulated with impunity by educational institutions, provided the institutions correctly define these categories of speech in their rules and identify these types of speech correctly in applying those rules.

Threats

A true threat, for which a person may be criminally prosecuted, is defined generally as a statement that would arouse in a reasonable person a fear of imminent bodily injury and is intended by the speaker to do so (*Virginia v. Black*, 538 U.S. 343, 359 [2003]). Thus, for example, a university could discipline a student for threatening Facebook posts even if these fell short of the true threat standard required for a criminal prosecution (*Tatro v. University of Minnesota*, 800 N.W.2d 811 [Minn. Ct. App. 2011]).

Fighting Words

Fighting words are statements that "tend to incite an immediate breach of the peace," where a "breach of the peace" means physical violence (*Gooding v. Wilson*, 405 U.S. 518, 521 [1972], quoting *Chaplinsky v. New Hamphire*, 315 U.S. 568 [1942]). Such statements are not protected speech under the First Amendment and may therefore be prohibited by campus authorities. Indeed, such speech may subject the speaker to criminal prosecution; for example, for disorderly conduct (e.g., *Mosley v. City of Auburn*, 428 So. 2d 165 [Ala. Crim. App. 1982]).

Speech that is merely offensive does not trigger the fighting words doctrine. In *UWM Post, Inc. v. Board of Regents of the University of Wisconsin System* (774 F. Supp. 1163 [E.D. Wis. 1991]), the university defended under the fighting words doctrine a speech policy that prohibited speech that was determined to be racist or demeaning to persons based on various characteristics. The court in *UWM* rejected the university's argument that the policy was limited to prohibiting fighting words, reasoning that speech that was prohibited by the policy could fall short of fighting words (*UWM* 1991, 1171).

However, the context of speech is important in determining whether speech constitutes unprotected fighting words. In *State v. Hoshijo* (76 P.3d 550 [Hawai'i 2003]), a student team manager who threatened and yelled racial slurs at a spectator during a basketball game exposed the university that employed him to liability under a state antidiscrimination law because the speech was likely to result in a violent reaction.

Defamation

A defamatory statement is a false statement of fact regarding the subject person that is made to another and that harms the subject's reputation (*Cwelinsky v. Mobil Chem. Co.*, 364 F.3d 68 [2nd Cir. 2004]). Libel is a written defamatory statement, and slander is a spoken one. Statements regarding public officials and other public figures that involve matters of public concern receive heightened protection under the First Amendment to encourage discussion of important public issues (*New York Times v. Sullivan*, 376 U.S. 254 [1964]; *Gertz v. Welch*, 418 U.S. 323 [1974]).

Campus speech by students, faculty, or administrators may give rise to defamation claims. In *Mazart v. New York* (109 Misc.2d 1092 [Ct. Cl. NY 1981]), a student newspaper published a prank letter in which the students falsely named as the authors of the letter identified themselves as "members of the gay community." However, statements by faculty and student witnesses in a plagiarism proceeding did not constitute slander where the statements were matters of opinion rather than fact or were true statements and thus not actionable (*Reardon v. Allegheny College*, 926 A.2d 477 [Pa. 2007]).

Speech Inciting Illegal Conduct

Speech that encourages illegal conduct can be prohibited if the speaker intends to incite others to engage in "imminent lawless action" and the speech, under the circumstances, is likely to succeed in doing so (*Brandenburg v. Ohio*, 395 U.S. 444, 448 [1969]). *Brandenburg*'s standard is a stringent one that permits criminal prosecutions for persons whose speech amounts to aiding and abetting criminal conduct. Brandenburg provides "almost completely free speech" (Penaro 2008, 266), and few instances of student speech are likely to fall into the category.

For example, in *Healey v. James* (408 U.S. 169 [1972]), students sought to form a chapter of Students for a Democratic Society, a group that engaged in protest activities regarding the war in Vietnam. The university refused to recognize the group because it was convinced that the group would disrupt educational activities on the campus. The Supreme Court, invoking *Brandenburg* as well as other authorities, agreed that the university's anticipation that the student group would encourage lawless conduct was insufficient reason to deny recognition on the grounds that such conduct was not protected speech.

Obscenity

The distribution of obscene material may be punished by criminal statutes. While obscenity may be prohibited by university speech policies, it is also sanctionable by criminal statutes and thus does not present special problems for campus speech. For purposes of the First Amendment, obscenity is speech that lacks "serious literary, artistic, political, or scientific value"; is "patently offensive"; and appeals primarily to a "prurient interest" in sex (*Miller v. California*, 413 U.S. 15 [1973]. Speech that is merely offensive because it includes explicit material may still receive protection under the First Amendment.

In *Papish v. Board of Curators of the University of Missouri* (410 U.S. 667 [1973]), a student was dismissed from a university for distributing an underground newspaper that included a political cartoon depicting the rape of the Statue of Liberty by police officers and profane language. The university's speech policy prohibited indecent speech, but the court held that the speech was protected because it did not rise to the level of obscenity. The court reasoned that the "mere dissemination of ideas—no matter how offensive to good taste—on a state university campus may not be shut off in the name alone of conventions of decency" (*Papish* 1973, 670).

FORMAL REQUIREMENTS OF POLICIES REGULATING SPEECH

The following are legal principles with which rules that regulate speech must comply. All but vagueness apply specifically to the First Amendment. Vagueness is a general requirement of due process that must be a feature of any valid law with a punitive sanction.

Prior Restraint

A prior restraint on speech is synonymous with censorship and characterizes any rule or policy that effectively prevents persons from engaging in speech activities. It is very unlikely that courts will approve a prior restraint on speech. As the court stated in *Bantam Books, Inc. v. Sullivan* (372 U.S. 58, 70 [1963]), "[a]ny system of prior restraints of expression comes to this Court bearing a heavy presumption against its constitutional validity."

Naturally, prohibitions on student speech constitute prior restraints. Thus, in *Widmar v. Vincent* (464 U.S. 263 [1981]), the Supreme Court held that a university's refusal to grant recognition to student religious groups for expressive activities, when the university granted such recognition to secular student groups, constituted an impermissible prior restraint on speech that violated the First Amendment (*Widmar* 1981, 267–68 and n. 5). Time, place, and manner restrictions on speech, discussed in further detail later, may also constitute prior restraints on speech that violate the First Amendment.

Overbreadth

A statute regulating speech is unconstitutionally overbroad on its face if it prohibits a substantial amount of protected speech as well as speech that is not protected by the First Amendment (*Houston v. Hill*, 482 U.S. 451, 458–60 [1985]). In *Doe v. University of Michigan* [721 F. Supp. 852 (1989), the court held that a university rule that prohibited "stigmatizing or victimizing" students on the basis of race, sex, religion, sexual orientation, and other categories was overbroad because it prohibited a substantial amount of protected speech.

Chilling Effect

A court is likely to find a regulation of speech unconstitutional if the rule is so drafted or framed that it has a "chilling effect" on protected speech in that it inhibits or discourages persons from engaging in speech protected by the First Amendment. This concept is closely related to overbreadth because an overbroad statute is likely to have the effect of discouraging protected speech activity. Nonetheless, a "chilling effect" is conceptually distinct from overbreadth.

Campus speech policies may be constitutionally defective if they have a chilling effect on speech, regardless of their intent. In *Husain v. Springer* (494 F.3d 108 [2nd Cir. 2007]), a college newspaper endorsed candidates in a student government election, prompting the college president to invalidate the results. The court, noting that the newspaper "scaled back its coverage of elections and reduced the prominence and extent of its candidate endorsements in an effort to avoid provoking another election nullification," found that the president's actions had a chilling effect on student speech that violated the First Amendment (*Husain* 2007, 128).

Vagueness

The concept of due process in the Fifth and Fourteenth Amendments to the U.S. Constitution requires that a law be drafted in such a manner that persons may reasonably be expected to understand what the law prohibits (*Broadrick v. Oklahoma*, 413 U.S. 601, 607 [1973]). In *Doe v. University of Michigan*, the court held that the university's speech policy prohibiting speech that "victimized" or "stigmatized" persons based on several characteristics was unconstitutionally vague because "these terms are general and elude precise definition" (*Doe* 1989, 867).

Content Discrimination

The First Amendment prohibits government restrictions on speech due to its content, and such restrictions are "presumptively invalid" (*United States v. Stevens*, 559 U.S. 460, 468 [2010]). The foregoing categories of speech that may be restricted based on their content, such as obscenity and fighting words, are narrow and limited exceptions to this general rule. Even within these categories of speech, moreover, government may not selectively restrict some instances of a category but not others, as this selective prohibition would amount to content discrimination in violation of the First Amendment.

The United States' robust protection for freedom of speech makes it difficult to for government to target hate speech, as compared to efforts to do so by other Western democracies (O'Neill 2012). Consequently, it is more difficult to regulate hateful or offensive campus speech in the United States than in Europe (Tsesis 2010). Advocates of such laws in the United States emphasize that they promote social equality but gloss over their purpose and effect, which is to regulate the content and viewpoint of speech (e.g., Waldron 2010), and that is what the First Amendment prohibits.

Campus speech policies seeking to avoid specific types of abusive or discriminatory speech may run afoul of the prohibition on content discrimination. For example, in *Iota Chi Chapter of Sigma Chi Fraternity v. George Mason University* (993 F.2d 386 [4th Cir. 1993]), a student group sponsored an entertainment event that included sexist and racially offensive costumes and skits. When students complained about the event, the university suspended the organization for the remainder of the academic year and imposed further sanctions on the group.

Noting that the fraternity was being punished for the ideas communicated by the skits and costumes, the court held that the punishments constituted content discrimination that violated the students' speech rights under the First Amendment (*Iota Chi* 1993, 392–93). While the court recognized the university's "substantial interest in maintaining an educational environment free of discrimination and racism, and in providing gender-neutral education," the court nonetheless concluded that this interest did not override the First Amendment's strictures against content discrimination in regulating speech (*Iota Chi* 1993, 393).

Viewpoint Discrimination

The First Amendment prohibits regulations aimed at prohibiting speech based on the viewpoint expressed, which is a specific type of content discrimination. Thus, for example, in *Rosenberger v. University of Virginia* (515 U.S. 819 [1995]), the Supreme Court held that a university that provided funds from student fees to student organizations could not exclude a student newspaper from receiving such funds on the ground that it expressed a religious point of view.

However, in *Christian Legal Society of the University of California, Hastings College of Law v. Martinez* (561 U.S. 661 [2010]), the Supreme Court held that a university's "accept all comers" policy requiring recognized student organizations to accept all students as members did not constitute viewpoint discrimination or otherwise violate the associative or religious rights of a religious student organization prohibited from excluding students from membership on the basis of factors that contravened the student group's religious beliefs, such as sexual orientation.

A significant distinction between *Rosenberger* and *Christian Legal Society* is that, in the latter, the university's regulation did not inhibit speech based on the viewpoint being expressed. On the contrary, the "accept all comers" policy did not directly regulate the speech of student organizations but only their membership policies. A policy that prohibited student groups from restricting membership on a selective class of specified characteristics, such as race, gender, and sexual orientation, was likewise held not to violate the First Amendment in *Alpha Delta Chi Delta Chapter v. Reed* (648 F.3d 790 [9th Cir. 2010]).

Time, Place, and Manner Restrictions

Expressive activities may often interfere with other legitimate activities persons have the lawful freedom to pursue. As a result, governments "may impose reasonable restrictions on the time, place, or manner of protected speech, provided the restrictions are justified without reference to the content of the regulated speech, that they are narrowly tailored to serve a significant governmental interest, and that they leave open ample alternative channels for communication of the information" (*Ward v. Rock Against Racism*, 498 U.S. 781, 791 [1989]).

There are categories of fora for purposes of time, place, and manner restrictions, each of which is relevant to campus speech policies. A traditional public forum is a place where one expects expressive activities to occur, such as a public park (*Arkansas Educ. Television Comm'n v. Forbes*, 523 U.S. 666, 676 [1998]). In a designated public forum, government has designated some property as available for speech purposes. Here, it must treat speech on the property the same way it would in a traditional public forum (*Forbes*, 523 U.S. at 677).

A limited public forum is one in which government permits speech activities to occur for certain groups or subjects (*Walker v. Texas Div., Sons of Confederate Veterans*, — U.S. —, 135 S.Ct. 2239, 2277 [2015]). Any limitations on the speech beyond those permitted in a traditional or designated public forum must be related to the other purposes for which the property is used, such as conducting classes on a school campus (*Good News Club v. Milford Central School*, 533 U.S., 105 [2001]).

A final category of forum for speech purposes is the nonpublic forum. A nonpublic forum is private property or public property not used for expressive activities, such as government buildings and offices. Content regulations on speech are permissible in nonpublic fora that are public property, provided the regulations relate to the purpose for which the property is used (*Forbes*, 523 at 676).

If campus officials seek to limit speech activities in some areas on campus, then they must do so clearly. In *OSU Student Alliance v. Ray* (699 F.3d 1033 [9th Cir. 2012]), a university had thrown away papers published by a conservative student group that the group had placed in bins alongside bins containing the university's student newspaper, claiming it had permitted the group to locate its papers in two designated spaces only. The court observed that state administrative regulations designated the campus a public forum "except for any grounds designated for authorized access only" (*OSU Student Alliance* quoting OAR 576-005-0015[1]). Due to the state's action, the campus in *OSU Student Alliance* was a designated public forum, and had the campus chosen to do so, it could have made some areas limited or nonpublic public fora pursuant to the state administrative rule. In this case, the university failed to do so because it had no written policy regarding the placement of newspaper bins. When the university disposed of the conservative group's bins and papers, it violated the students' First Amendment rights because the university, which gave a preference to the official student newspaper for the university, engaged in viewpoint discrimination (*OSU Student Alliance* 2012, 1066–67).

Roberts v. Haragan (346 F. Supp.2d 853 [N.D. Tex. 2004]) illustrates issues that may arise with respect to the designation of certain areas of a campus as "free speech zones." In *Roberts*, a student wanted to speak and distribute literature outside of designated "free speech areas" of a university campus and was denied permission to do so by campus authorities. The court observed that the university's speech policies, by designating some spaces as "free speech areas," could not impose limitations on speech in those areas beyond those prohibiting unprotected categories of speech and reasonable time, place, and manner restrictions. The speech code in *Roberts* could not be constitutionally applied to speech in spaces that were designated or limited public fora because the code subjected students to discipline who engaged in speech that is protected by the First Amendment (*Roberts* 2012, 872). The court observed that, while the university had a defensible rationale for imposing the strictures of its speech code in the classroom, where the university conducted its core mission, that rationale did not extend to public fora on the campus, including designated and limited public fora, where speech had to receive the fullest protection of the First Amendment (*Roberts* 2012, 871–73).

STATUTORY RESTRICTIONS ON SPEECH

Federal and civil rights statutes impose limitations on speech, and college administrators are bound to comply with these laws. Title VII of the Civil Rights Act of 1964 prohibits discrimination on the basis of race, color, sex, national origin, and religion, which includes discrimination in educational opportunities. Title IX of the Education Amendments of 1972 forbids sex discrimination in education for schools that receive federal funds (20 U.S.C. § 1681[a]). Schools, both public and private, are potentially subject to hostile environment claims under Title VII. To prevail on a claim that they have suffered unlawful discrimination in violation of Title VII or Title IX, a plaintiff must show that he or she has been "subjected to harassment severe enough to compromise the victim's employment or educational opportunities and, in the case of a Title IX claim (but not under Title VII), the institution must have had actual knowledge of the harassment and have exhibited deliberate indifference to it [citation omitted]" (*Wills v. Brown University*, 184 F.3d 20, 26 [1st Cir. 1999]).

Campus speech regulations may clearly be directed to avoiding liability under these federal statutes or state civil rights statutes. These statutes may not exceed the limitations permitted under the First Amendment. Thus, for example, in *Dejohn v. Temple University* (537 F.3d 301 [3d Cir. 2008]), a student claimed that a campus speech policy violated his First Amendment rights by preventing him from expressing his views regarding the role of women in the military. The speech policy in *Dejohn* prohibited "expressive, visual or physical conduct of a sexual or gender-motivated nature when . . . (c) such conduct has the purpose or effect of unreasonably interfering with an individual's work, educational performance, or status; or (d) such conduct has the purpose or effect of creating an intimidating, hostile, or offensive environment." The court held that the policy was facially overbroad in violation of the First Amendment because it prohibited protected speech.

Likewise, in *College Republicans at San Francisco State University v. Reed* (523 F. Supp.2d 1005 [N.D. Cal. 2007]), a student organization held an event in which the students abused Islamic symbols, and they claimed that the university violated their First Amendment rights by charging them with misconduct in violation of a speech code that prohibited speech that was not "civil" or that was inconsistent with the university's "goals, principles, and policies." While the speech involved in that case was protected under the First Amendment, it did not create a hostile environment under federal civil rights statutes. That speech would be deemed offensive by many was insufficient to permit the university to prohibit the speech in *College Republicans*. However, a college permissibly dismissed an instructor who had given a gay student religious pamphlets reflecting her views on homosexuality (*Pigee v. Carl Sandburg College*, 464 F.3d 667 [7th Cir. 2006]). Likewise, a court held that an instructor could be disciplined for creating a hostile environment for his use of profanity and discussion of sexual matters in class (*Cohen v. San Bernardino Valley College*, 883 F. Supp. 1407 [C.D. Cal. 1995]).

A general speech policy that prohibits offensive speech on campus is more likely to be found overbroad because it prohibits speech protected by the First Amendment. A court is more likely to find conduct that creates a hostile environment under Title VII or Title IX when the conduct is personal, as in *Pigee*, or pervasive and repeated, as in *Cohen*. Observers who recommend speech codes to address offensive conduct recognize that speech is more likely to be sanctionable consistent with the First Amendment when it involves inequality in power relations, as between faculty and students, or is pervasive in nature (Earle and Cava 1997).

PROMOTING EDUCATIONAL GOALS BY PROTECTING FREEDOM OF SPEECH

Speech codes and regulations of campus speech that prevent speech that insults or offends students are intended to enable the college or university to avoid liability under state and federal laws that forbid discrimination against classes of persons that have historically suffered from unlawful and unjust discrimination in the United States. Campus authorities must comply with these laws as a matter of fact, and the existence of these laws evidences that it is the will of the public that they do so.

In addition, such rules are intended to shield students from insensitive, harassing, and offensive speech to establish and preserve learning environ- ments in which students can focus on their studies free from speech and conduct that would marginalize them and distract them from the business of acquiring an education, which it is the core mission of colleges and univer- sities. This is rationally defensible because campuses must have rules that enable them to perform their essential functions. No one could approve of educational institutions inviting students to attend campuses where they will be abused.

A review of the law governing campus speech, however, shows that campuses are not unidimensional spaces. Some portions of a college campus, such as classrooms, libraries, and labs that are dedicated to instruction and study, have a purpose restricted to educational activities that require some limitations on expression to perform their educational function for students. Such restrictions do not violate the First Amendment. Other parts of cam- puses, including quads, greenways, sidewalks, and streets, do not have such purposes, and there is no legal justification for limiting speech in such spaces beyond those limitations permitted in other public fora.

The recent invention of free speech zones is best understood as an effort to relegate dissent to a few confined spaces where it can be conveniently ignored (Allen 2011). Campus authorities run into trouble when they extend the speech restrictions appropriate to the classroom to other spaces where we should expect expressive activities to occur. This is the conundrum adminis- trators face: How do we protect students from abusive speech that would impede their learning but at the same time protect the freedom of speech not only mandated by law but that also lies at the heart of our representative system of government and civil liberties?

Thankfully, the law itself supplies an answer to the apparent dilemma administrators must address. The First Amendment provides robust protec- tion for freedom of expression and binds administrators to limit speech activ- ities no more than is permitted to allow protected speech to occur on those portions of a campus where one would expect students and the public to conduct such activities. Campus authorities may prohibit speech that is not protected by the First Amendment, and they may impose reasonable time, place, and manner restrictions on speech.

Here, speech codes that impose limitations on speech beyond those authorized by the First Amendment are not only inappropriate but also illegal. However, administrators may limit or prohibit expression in parts of a campus that are nonpublic fora, such as classrooms, libraries, offices, and the like, that are dedicated to educational and administrative functions where one does not expect freedom of expression. Here, limitations on speech that prohibit harassing, offensive, and abusive speech are not only permissible but also consistent with the institution's educational mission and may be, moreover, mandated by civil rights statutes. This multidimensional regime of rules for the regulation of speech promotes education. In the classroom, students learn their subjects of study. On the broader campus, they mature into educated adults prepared to live, compete, and thrive in a world that is not always agreeable.

CONCLUSION

The instructors' task is to help students to learn the subject matter and, more fundamentally, to develop the skills that will make them better students and to prepare for their careers and citizenship in our society. The classroom must be a place in which students can focus on their study, and students should be able to express themselves consistent with maintaining an environment conducive to learning and dialogue. A campus is a community that is broader than the classroom, and it mirrors the diversity of persons and views that reflects broad society.

Outside the classroom, students should expect to be exposed to the range of views and speech that they will encounter when they graduate and enter the workforce and participate in our society and politics, and this is a part of the students' education. Existing law on campus speech reflects this perspective.

The classroom and other portions of a campus dedicated to learning and administration are not public fora, and there, the law and administrators may impose reasonable restrictions on speech consistent with the functions of those spaces. Other spaces on the campus are public fora, and there, the fullest expression authorized by the U.S. Constitution must be respected.

Appendix

Oral Rubric Combined with Rubric for
Written Assignment

Desired Skills to be Assessed	Comments	/pts
Evaluating the Oral Presentation		
1. Identification, framing and introduction of the issue. Does the issue receive proper introduction? Is it presented in a way that makes the audience understand the importance of the material? Is the issue placed within its proper context? Why should we care about this?		/5
2. Development of the idea from introduction through supporting argumentation to the conclusion. Does the argument logically cohere? Is the conclusion supported by what preceded it? Are the transitions between points understandable? Do you present it sequentially so that people "get it?"		/10
3. How well has the debate identified and used primary sources to support the argument? Is the argument based on facts or emotion? Have you given the audience adequate basis to evaluate your sources?		/5
4. Presentation. This encompasses: a) Appropriate use of power point text and images b) Use of language c) Body language (do you spend the entire time with your back turned to the class reading off the screen? If so, very bad) d) Do you engage students, and leave room for questions? e) 5. Does the presentation go for the assigned 7.5 minutes, or does it go well under or over the allocated time?		/10

Evaluating the Paper		
1. Identification, framing and introduction of the issue. Does the issue receive proper introduction? Does the paper present it in a way that the reader understands what the paper will be about, what it hopes to prove, and why the issue is significant?		/5
2. Proper use of sources. This ranges from the quality of sources consulted to the proper citation of sources. (If you have any doubts – even after I've talked about this in class – please ask any professor. We are happy to give help when it comes to properly citing sources) Care should be taken to make certain that web sites are credible and, to the extent possible, have undergone editing or review from outside sources. Note that websites affiliated with governmental or university entities are often more reliable, but that does not make them automatically accurate. Have you relied on eye-witness testimony, primary sources, or opinions? None are free from bias, but eye witness testimony offers a first-hand account.		/10
3. Development of the idea from thesis statement (what you hope to prove) to supporting documentation and argumentation to a proper conclusion. Has the paper proven what it set out to prove – within reasonable bounds? Is the paper logical and clear in its development?		/10
4. Use of proper grammar, punctuation, spelling, and the elimination of written "infelicities" so far as possible.		/5
Additional Comments:	Total points: /60	

References

Abes, Elisa S., Susan R. Jones, and Marylu K. McEwen. 2007. "Reconceptualizing the Model of Multiple Dimensions of Identity: The Role of Meaning-Making Capacity in the Construction of Multiple Identities." *Journal of College Student Development* 48 (1): 1–22.

Allen, David S. 2011. "Spatial Frameworks and the Management of Dissent: From Parks to Free Speech Zones." *Communication Law and Policy* 16 (Autumn): 383–423.

Allison, Donnetrice C. 2008. "Free to Be Me? Black Professors, White Institutions." *Journal of Black Studies* 38 (4): 641–62.

American Council on the Teaching of Foreign Languages. n.d. *Standards for Foreign Language Learning: Preparing for the 21st Century.* Accessed June 28, 2016. https://assessment.trinity.duke.edu/documents/StandardsforForeignLanguageLearning.pdf.

Angelo, Thomas A., and Patricia K. Cross. 1993. *Classroom Assessment Techniques.* San Francisco: Jossey-Bass.

Archdeacon, Thomas J. 1985. "Problems and Possibilities in the Study of American Immigration and Ethnic History." *International Migration Review* 19 (1): 112–34.

Ashworth, Gregory J., and Rudi Hartmann, eds. 2005. *Horror and Human Tragedy Revisited: The Management of Sites of Atrocities for Tourism.* New York: Cognizant Communication.

Austen, Jane. 2014. *Pride and Prejudice.* New York: Millennium.

Avery, Derek R., and Kecia M. Thomas. 2004. "Blending Content and Contact: The Roles of Diversity Curriculum and Campus Heterogeneity in Fostering Diversity Management Competency." *Academy of Management Learning and Education* 3 (4): 380–96.

Banks, James A. 2002. *An Introduction to Multicultural Education.* 3rd ed. Boston: Allyn and Bacon.

Barr, Joseph. 2013. "Discussing Gender and Sexuality in the Community College Classroom." *Inquiry: The Journal of the Virginia Community Colleges* 18 (1): 13–19.

Berger, Michele Tracy, and Kathleen Guidroz, eds. 2009. *The Intersectional Approach: Transforming the Academy through Race, Class and Gender.* Chapel Hill: University of North Carolina Press.

Bischoping, Katherine. 2004. "*Timor mortis conturbat me*: Genocide Pedagogy and Vicarious Trauma." *Journal of Genocide Research* 6 (4): 545–66.

Blum, Lawrence. 2004. "The Poles, the Jews and the Holocaust: Reflections on an AME Trip to Auschwitz." *Journal of Moral Education* 33 (2): 131–48.

Bower, Beverly L. 2002. "Campus Life for Faculty of Color: Still Strangers after All These Years?" In *Community College Faculty: Characteristics, Practices, and Challenges*, edited by Charles Outcalt, 79–88. San Francisco: Jossey-Bass.

Boyer, Paul S., Clifford E. Clark, Karen Halttunen, Joseph Kett, Neal Salisbury, Harvard Sitkoff, and Nancy Woloch. 2011. *The Enduring Vision: A History of the American People.* Vol. 2. 7th edition. New York: Wadsworth.

Brackett, Marc A., and Susan E. Rivers. 2014. "Transforming Students' Lives with Social and Emotional Learning." In *International Handbook of Emotions in Education*, edited by Reinhard Pekrun and Lisa Linnenbrink-Garcia, 1–3, 368–88. New York: Taylor and Francis.

Broder, Henryk. 2014. "Auschwitz ist heute ein Disneyland des Todes." *Die Welt*, January 27. Accessed June 27, 2016. http://www.welt.de/kultur/article124251623/Auschwitz-ist-heute-ein-Disneyland-des-Todes.html.

Brown, Ted, dir. 2008. *Darfur Now: Six Stories, One Hope.* Burbank, CA: Warner Home Video, DVD.

Buckley, Charles A. 2011. "Student and Staff Perceptions of the Research-Teaching Nexus." *Innovations in Education and Teaching International* 48 (3): 313–22.

Bussema, Evelyn, and Pat Nemec. 2006. "Training to Increase Cultural Competence." *Psychiatric Rehabilitation Journal* 30 (1): 71–72.

Butcher, Charity. 2012. "Teaching Foreign Policy Decision Making Processes Using Role-Playing Simulations: The Case of U.S.–Iranian Relations." *International Studies Perspectives* 13 (2): 176–94.

Carmigian, Patrick R. 2013. "Seeing through Lies: Teaching Ideological Literacy as a Corrective Lens." *Equity and Excellence in Education* 46 (1): 119–34.

Cetin, Fethiye. 2012. *My Grandmother: A Memoir.* Brooklyn, NY: Verso.

Chrobot-Mason, Donna. 2004. "Managing Racial Differences: The Role of Majority Managers' Ethnic Identity Development on Minority Employee Perceptions of Support." *Group Organization Management* 29 (1): 5–31.

Clyde, Carol. 2010. "Developing Civic Leaders through an Experiential Learning Program for Holocaust Education." *Prospects* 40 (2): 289–306.

Clyde, Carol L., David A. Walker, and Deborah L. Floyd. 2005. "An Experiential Learning Program for Holocaust Education." *Journal of Student Affairs, Research and Practice* 42 (3): 588–603.

Cohen, Stephen. 2006. *The Idea of Pakistan.* Washington, DC: Brookings Institution Press.

Cole, Tim. 2000. *Selling the Holocaust: From Auschwitz to Schindler—How History Is Bought, Packaged, and Sold.* New York: Routledge.

Collings, Deirdre, and Rafal Rohozinski. 2009. *Bullets and Blogs: New Media and the Warfighter.* Carlisle, PA: U.S. Army War College, Centre for Strategic Leadership. Accessed June 29, 2016. http://www.dtic.mil/cgi-bin/GetTRDoc?Location=U2&doc=GetTRDoc.pdf&AD=ADA508195.

Cowan, Paula, and Henry Maitles. 2011. "'We Saw Inhumanity Close Up': What Is Gained by School Students from Scotland Visiting Auschwitz?" *Journal of Curriculum Studies* 43 (2): 163–84.

Crenshaw, Kimberlé. 1989. "Demarginalizing the Intersection of Race and Sex: A Black Feminist Critique of Antidiscrimination Doctrine, Feminist Theory and Anti-Racist Politics." *University of Chicago Legal Forum* 140: 139–67.

———. 1991. "Mapping the Margins: Intersectionality, Identity Politics, and Violence against Women of Color." *Stanford Law Review* 43 (6): 1241–99.

Curtis, Polly, and Martin Hodgson. 2008. "Student Researching al-Qaida Tactics Held for Six Days." *Guardian*, May 24. Accessed June 29, 2016. http://www.theguardian.com/education/2008/may/24/highereducation.uk.

Daniels, Roger. 2002. *Coming to America: A History of Immigration and Ethnicity in American Life.* 2nd edition. New York: Harper Perennial.

Dawson, Bryan L., and Michael J. Goren. 2011. "State of the Art: How Diversity Training Research Informs Practice." Paper presented at the symposium Diversity Training: Linking Theory and Practice, Society for Industrial and Organizational Psychology annual conference, Chicago, IL, April.

Dearborn, Mary. 1988. *Love in the Promised Land: The Story of Anzia Yezierska.* New York: Free Press.

Deardorff, Darla K. 2006. "Identification and Assessment of Intercultural Competence as a Student Outcome of Internationalization." *Journal of Studies in International Education* 10 (3): 241–66.

Dill, Bonnie Thornton. 2002. "Work at the Intersections of Race, Gender, Ethnicity, and Other Dimensions of Difference in Higher Education." *Connections: Newsletter of the Consortium on Race, Gender, and Ethnicity* (Fall): 5–7.

Dill, Bonnie Thornton, Amy McLaughlin, and Angel Davis Nieves. 2007. "Future Directions of Feminist Research: Intersectionality." In *Handbook of Feminist Research*, edited by Sharlene N. Hesse-Biber, 629–37. Thousand Oaks, CA: Sage.

Dill, Bonnie T., and Ruth E. Zambrana, eds. 2009. *Emerging Intersections. Race, Class and Gender in Theory, Policy, and Practice.* New Brunswick, NJ: Rutgers University Press.

Doyle, Elaine, and Patrick Buckley. 2014. "Research Ethics in Teaching and Learning." *Innovations in Education and Teaching International* 51 (2): 153–63.

Du Bois, W. E. B. 1952. "The Negro and the Warsaw Ghetto." *Jewish Life* 6 (7): 14–15.

Eagan, Kevin, Ellen Bara Stolzenberg, Joseph J. Ramirez, Melissa C. Aragon, Maria Ramirez Suchard, and Cecilia Rios-Aguilar. 2016. *The American Freshman: Fifty-Year Trends 1966–2015.* Expanded ed. Los Angeles: Higher Education Research Institute.

Earle, Beverly, and Anita Cava. 1997. "The Collision of Rights and a Search for Limits: Free Speech in the Academy and Freedom from Sexual Harassment on Campus." *Berkeley Journal of Employment and Labor Law* 18 (April): 282–322.

Egoyan, Atom, dir. 2003. *Ararat.* Cambridge, MA: Miramax, DVD.

Engel, Susan. 2013. "The Case for Curiosity." *Educational Leadership* 70 (5): 37–38.

Ferdman, Bernardo M. 2003a. "Key Principles for Building Diversity and Inclusion." *California Psychologist* 36 (6): 11–12.

———. 2003b. "Learning about Our and Others' Selves: Multiple Identities and Their Sources." In *Crossing Cultures: Insights from Master Teachers*, edited by Nakiye Boyacigiller, Richard A. Goodman, and Margaret E. Phillips, 49–61. New York: Routledge.

———. 2010. "Teaching Inclusion by Example and Experience: Creating an Inclusive Learning Environment." In *Leading across Differences: Cases and Perspectives—Facilitator's Guide*, edited by Kelly M. Hannum, Belinda McFeeters, and Lize Booysen, 37–49. San Francisco: Pfeiffer.

Fink, L. Dee. 2003. *Creating Significant Learning Experiences.* San Francisco: Jossey-Bass.

Finkelstein, Norman G. 2000. *The Holocaust Industry: Reflections on the Exploitation of Jewish Suffering.* 1st edition. New York: Verso Books.

Fleisher, Belton, Hashimoto Masinori, and Bruce A. Weinberg. 2002. "Foreign GTAs Can Be Effective Teachers of Economics." *Journal of Economic Education* 33 (4): 299–325.

Foner, Eric. 2011. *Give Me Liberty: An American Promise.* Vol. 2. New York: W. W. Norton.

Fong, Rowena. 2004. "Contexts and Environments for Culturally Competent Practice." In *Culturally Competent Practice with Immigrant and Refugee Children and Families*, edited by Rowena Fong, 39–59. New York: Guilford Press.

Foster, Stuart J. 1999. "Using Historical Empathy to Excite Students about the Study of History: Can You Empathize with Neville Chamberlain?" *Social Studies* 90 (1): 18–24.

Fowler, Michael R. 2009. "Culture and Negotiation: The Pedagogical Dispute Regarding Cross-Cultural Simulations." *International Studies Perspectives* 10 (3): 341–59.

Freeden, Michael. 2016. "The Resurgence of Ideology Studies: Twenty Years of the JPI." *Journal of Political Ideologies* 21 (1): 1–8.

Freire, Paulo. 1998. *Pedagogy of Freedom: Ethics, Democracy and Civic Courage.* Lanham, MD: Rowman and Littlefield.

Gahungu, Athanase. 2011. "Integration of Foreign-Born Faculty in Academia: Foreignness as an Asset." *International Journal of Educational Leadership Preparation* 6 (1): 1–22.

Gallagher, Ryan. 2011. "Two Arrests, a Suspension, Accusations of Islamophobia: Nottingham University Must Submit to a Public Enquiry." *Open Democracy*, May 13. Accessed June 29, 2016. https://www.opendemocracy.net/ourkingdom/ryan-gallagher/two-arrests-suspension-accusations-of-islamophobia-nottingham-university-m.

Gallagher-Geurtsen, Tricia. 2009. "Inspiring Hybridity: A Call to Engage with(in) Global Flows of the Multicultural Classroom." *Multicultural Perspectives* 11 (4): 200–203.

Gannett, Ruth Stiles. 1948. *My Father's Dragon*. New York: Random House.

General Accounting Office. 2014. "Issues Related to State Voter Identification Laws." *GAO.gov*. Accessed on June 28, 2016. http://www.gao.gov/products/GAO-14-634.

Gerdes, Karen E., Elizabeth A. Segal, Kelly Jackson, and Jennifer L. Mullins. 2011. "Teaching Empathy: A Framework Rooted in Social Cognitive Neuroscience and Social Justice." *Journal of Social Work Education* 47 (1): 109–31.

Gill, John. 2011. "Police Pay £20k to Nottingham Student Arrested over Terror Manual." *Times Higher Education*, September 15. Accessed June 29, 2016. https://www.timeshighereducation.com/news/police-pay-20k-to-nottingham-student-arrested-over-terror-manual/417477.article.

Goldberg, Suzanne B. 2009. "Intersectionality in Theory and Practice." In *Intersectionality and Beyond: Law, Power and the Politics of Location*, edited by Emily Grabham, Davina Cooper, Jane Krishnadas, and Didi Herman, 124–58. Abbington, Oxon: Routledge-Cavendish.

Goldstein, Joshua, and Jon Pevehouse. *International Relations*. 10th edition. London: Pearson, 2013.

Gray, Michael. 2014. *Contemporary Debates in Holocaust Education*. Houndmills, UK: Palgrave Macmillan.

Griswold, Kim, Luis Zayas, Joan B. Kernan, and Christine M. Wagner. 2007. "Cultural Awareness through Medical Student and Refugee Patient Encounters." *Journal of Immigrant Health* 9 (1): 55–60.

Gutiérrez, Lorraine, Jean M. Kruzich, Teresa Jones, and Nora Coronado. 2000. "Identifying Goals and Outcome Measures for Diversity Training: A Multi-Dimensional Framework for Decision-Makers." *Administration in Social Work* 24 (3): 53–70.

Hadley, Alice Omaggio. 1993. *Teaching Language in Context*. Boston: Heinle and Heinle.

Hancock, Ange-Marie. 2007. "When Multiplication Doesn't Equal Quick Addition: Examining Intersectionality as a Research Paradigm." *Perspectives on Politics* 5 (1): 63–79.

Handlin, Oscar. 1951. *The Uprooted: The Epic Story of the Great Migrations That Made the American People*. Boston: Little Brown.

Harris, Tina M. 2007. "Black Feminist Thought and Cultural Contracts: Understanding the Intersection and Negotiation of Racial, Gendered, and Professional Identities in the Academy." In *Neither White nor Male: Female Faculty of Color*, edited by Katherine G. Hendrix, 55–64. San Francisco, CA: Jossey-Bass.

Hemley, Robin. 2015. *A Field Guide for Immersion Writing: Memoir, Journalism, and Travel*. Athens: University of Georgia Press.

Hite, Linda M., and Kimberly S. McDonald. 2006. "Diversity Training Pitfalls and Possibilities: An Exploration of Small and Mid-Size US Organizations." *Human Resource Development International* 9 (3): 365–77.

Hoffman, Jan. 2015. "Anxiety on Campus: Reporter's Notebook." *New York Times*, May 28. Accessed June 27, 2016. http://www.nytimes.com/times-insider/2015/05/28/anxiety-on-campus-reporters-notebook/?_r=0.

hooks, bell. 1994. *Teaching to Transgress: Education as the Practice of Freedom*. London: Routledge.

Hopper, E. Mason. 1922. *Hungry Hearts*. Samuel Goldwyn Films, 13:45. Accessed June 27, 2016. http://vimeo.com/9346999.

Hyde, Cheryl A. 1998. "A Model for Diversity Training in Human Services Agencies." *Administration in Social Work* 22 (4): 19–31.

Jefferson, Margo. 2015. *Negroland: A Memoir*. New York: Pantheon Books.

Joughin, Gordon. n.d. *A Short Guide to Oral Assessment*. Accessed June 27, 2016. https://www.leedsmet.ac.uk/publications/files/100317_36668_ShortGuideOralAssess1_WEB.pdf.

———. 1998. "Dimensions of Oral Assessment." *Assessment and Evaluation in Higher Education* 23 (4): 367–78.

Joughin, Gordon, and Gillian Collom. 2003. "Oral Assessment." *Biomedical Scientist* 47 (10): 1078–80.

Journell, Wayne. 2009. "Setting Out the (Un)Welcome Mat: A Portrayal of Immigration in State Standards for American History." *Social Studies* 100 (4): 160–68.

Kalpokas, Ignas. 2016. "Influence Operations: Challenging the Social Media—Democracy Nexus." *SAIS Europe Journal of Global Affairs* 19 (1): 18–29.

Kansteiner, Wulf. 2014. "Genocide Memory, Digital Cultures, and the Anesthetization of Violence." *Memory Studies* 7 (4): 403–8.

Kavas, Aysel, and Alican Kavas. 2008. "An Exploratory Study of Undergraduate College Students' Perceptions and Attitudes toward Foreign Accented Faculty." *College Student Journal* 42 (3): 879–90.

Kidd, David C., and Emmanuele Castano. 2013. "Reading Literary Fiction Improves Theory of Mind." *Science* 342 (6156): 377–80.

Kinkead, Joyce. 2003. "Learning through Inquiry: An Overview of Undergraduate Research." *New Directions for Teaching and Learning* 93 (March): 5–17.

Kirk, Delaney J., and Rita Durant. 2010. "Crossing the Line: Framing Appropriate Responses in the Diversity Classroom." *Journal of Management Education* 34 (6): 823–47.

Kirkpatrick, Donald. L. 1959. "Techniques for Evaluating Training Programs." *Journal of ASTD* 13: 1–13.

Kitzinger, Celia, and Elizabeth Peel. 2005. "The De-Gaying and Re-Gaying of AIDS: Contested Homophobias in Lesbian and Gay Awareness Training." *Discourse and Society* 16 (2): 173–97.

Knowles, Malcolm S., Elwood F. Holton III, and Richard A. Swanson. 1998. *The Adult Learner*. 5th ed. Woburn, MA: Butterworth-Heinemann.

Krain, Matthew, and Jeffrey S. Lantis. 2006. "Building Knowledge? Evaluating the Effectiveness of the Global Problems Summit Simulation." *International Studies Perspectives* 7 (4): 395–407.

Kranz, Tomasz, ed. 2013. *Educational Visits to the State Museum at Majdanek: A Guide for Teachers*. Lublin: Państwowe Muzeum na Majdanku.

Kulik, Carol T., Molly B. Pepper, Loriann Roberson, and Sharon K. Parker. 2007. "The Rich Get Richer: Predicting Participation in Voluntary Diversity Training." *Journal of Organizational Behavior* 28 (6): 753–69.

Lange-Ionatamishvili, Elina, and Sandra Svetoka. 2015. *Strategic Communications and Social Media in the Ukraine Russia Conflict*. Riga: NATO Strategic Communication Centre of Excellence. Accessed June 29, 2016. http://www.stratcomcoe.org/download/file/fid/2656.

Lantis, Jeffrey S., Kent J. Kille, and Matthew Krain. 2010. "The State of the Active Teaching and Learning Literature." In *The International Studies Encyclopedia*, vol. 10, edited by Robert Denemark. Hoboken, NJ: Blackwell Publishing. Blackwell Reference Online. http://www.isacompendium.com/subscriber/tocnode.html?id=g9781444336597_yr2015_chunk_g978144433659718_ss1-11.

Laswell, Harold D. 1936. *Who Gets What, When, How*. New York: Whittlesey House.

Law, Carolyn Leste. 1995. Introduction to *This Fine Place So Far from Home: Voices of Academics from the Working Class*, edited by C. L. Barney Dews and Carolyn Leste Law, 1–3. Philadelphia: Temple University Press.

Lee, Amy, Robert Poch, Marta Shaw, and Rhiannon D. Williams. 2012. *Engaging Diversity in Undergraduate Classrooms: A Pedagogy for Developing Intercultural Competence*: ASHE Higher Education Report. Hoboken, NJ: Wiley.

Lee, Changuk, and Kye-Sung Chon. 2000. "An Investigation of Multicultural Training Practices in the Restaurant Industry: The Training Cycle Approach." *International Journal of Contemporary Hospitality Management* 12 (2): 126–34.

Leming, Robert S. 1991. "Teaching the Law Using United States Supreme Court Cases." *ERIC Digest* (September). Accessed June 28, 2016. http://eric.ed.gov/?id=ED339673.

Lennon, John, and Malcolm Foley. 2000. *Dark Tourism*. London: Continuum.

Lippi-Green, Rosina. 1997. *English with an Accent: Language, Ideology, and Discrimination in the United States*. New York: Routledge.

Löfström, Erika. 2011. "'Does Plagiarism Mean Anything? LOL': Students' Conceptions of Writing and Citing." *Journal of Academic Ethics* 9 (4): 257–75.

Louie, Belinda. 2005. "Development of Empathetic Responses with Multicultural Literature." *Journal of Adolescent and Adult Literacy* 48 (7): 566–78.

Malveaux, Julianne. 2002. "Intersectionality: Big Words for Small Lives." *Black Issues in Higher Education* 19 (12): 27.

Manglitz, Elaine, Talmadge C. Guy, and Lisa R. Merriweather. 2014. "Knowledge and Emotions in Cross-Racial Dialogues: Changes and Opportunities for Adult Educators Committed to Racial Justice in Educational Settings." *Adult Learning* 25 (3): 111–18.

Mani, Anandi, Sendhil Mullainathan, Eldar Shafir, and Jiaying Zhao. 2013. "Poverty Impedes Cognitive Function." *Science* 341 (6149): 976–80.

McCall, Leslie. 2005. "The Complexity of Intersectionality." *Signs* 30 (3): 1771–1800.

———. 2009. "The Complexity of Intersectionality." In *Intersectionality and Beyond: Law, Power and the Politics of Location*, edited by Emily Grabham, Davina Cooper, Jane Krishnadas, and Didi Herman, 49–75. New York: Routledge-Cavendish.

McCroskey, Lynda L. 2002. "Domestic and International College Instructors: An Examination of Perceived Differences and Their Correlates." *Journal of Intercultural Communication Research* 31 (2): 63–83.

McCully, Alan. 2012. "History Teaching, Conflict and the Legacy of the Past." *Citizenship and Social Justice* 7 (2): 145–59.

McDougall, Andrew. 2015. "Asia's Skin Whitening Market Is Often Misunderstood." February 20. Accessed June 26, 2016. http://www.cosmeticsdesign-asia.com/Market-Trends/Asia-s-skin-whitening-market-is-often-misunderstood.

McIntosh, Peggy. 1993. "White Privilege and Male Privilege: A Personal Account of Coming to See Correspondences through Work in Women's Studies." In *Gender Basics: Feminist Perspectives on Women and Men*, edited by Bann Minas, 30–38. Belmont, CA: Wadsworth.

Mestenhauser, Josef A. 1983. "Learning from Sojourners." In *Handbook of Intercultural Training*, vol. 2, edited by Daniel Landis and Richard W. Brislin, 153–85. New York: Pergamon.

Migration Policy Institute. n.d. *Georgia Social and Demographics Fact Sheet*. Accessed on June 27, 2016. http://www.migrationpolicy.org/data/state-profiles/state/demographics/GA.

Milne, Alan Alexander. 2014. *Winnie-the-Pooh*. New York: Penguin.

Mingst, Karen A., and Ivan M. Arreguin-Toft. 2013. *Essentials of International Relations*. 6th ed. New York: W. W. Norton.

Modaff, John, and Robert Hopper. 1984. "Why Speech Is Basic." *Communication Education* 33 (1): 37–42.

Muzzin, Linda, and Lawrence Hart. 1985. "Oral Assessment." In *Assessing Clinical Competence*, edited by Victor Neufeld and Geoffrey Norman, 71–93. New York: Springer.

Nadal, Kevin L. 2013. *That's So Gay! Microaggressions and the Lesbian, Gay, Bisexual and Transgender Community*. Washington, DC: American Psychological Association.

National Public Radio (NPR). n.d. "Code Switch: Frontiers on Race, Culture and Ethnicity." Accessed June 26, 2016. http://www.npr.org/sections/codeswitch.

NATO STRATCOM. 2015a. *Analysis of Russia's Information Campaign against Ukraine*. Riga: NATO Strategic Communication Centre of Excellence. Accessed June 29, 2016. http://www.stratcomcoe.org/download/file/fid/3213.

———. 2015b. *DAESH Information Campaign and Its Influence: Results of the Study*. Riga: NATO Strategic Communication Centre of Excellence. Accessed June 29, 2016. http://www.stratcomcoe.org/daesh-information-campaign-and-its-influence-1.

———. 2015c. *Internet Trolling as a Hybrid Warfare Tool: The Case of Latvia*. Riga: NATO Strategic Communication Centre of Excellence. Accessed June 29, 2016. http://www.stratcomcoe.org/internet-trolling-hybrid-warfare-tool-case-latvia-0.

Neuliep, James W., and James C. McCroskey. 1997. "The Development of Intercultural and Interethnic Communication Apprehension Scales." *Communication Research Reports* 14 (2): 145–56.

Norman, Richard. 2012. "Worldviews, Humanism and the (Im)possibility of Neutrality." *Oxford Review of Education* 38 (5): 515–25.

O'Neill, Robert M. 2012. "Hate Speech, Fighting Words and Beyond: Why American Law Is Unique." *Albany Law Review* 76 (September): 467–98.

Ong, Walter. 1988. *Orality and Literacy*. New York: Routledge.

Papadatou-Pastou, Marietta, Maryanne Martin, Marcus R. Munafò, and Gregory V. Jones. 2008. "Sex Differences in Left-Handedness: A Meta-Analysis of 144 Studies." *Psychological Bulletin* 134 (5): 677–99.

Patitu, Carol L., and Kandace G. Hinton. 2003. "The Experiences of African American Women Faculty and Administrators in Higher Education: Has Anything Changed?" In *Meeting the Needs of African American Women*, edited by Mary F. Howard-Hamilton, 79–93. San Francisco: Jossey-Bass.

Patton, Lori D., and Christopher Catching. 2009. "'Teaching while Black': Narratives of African American Student Affairs Faculty." *International Journal of Qualitative Studies in Education* 22 (6): 713–28.

Penaro, Steven. 2008. "Reconciling Morse with Brandenburg." *Fordham Law Review* 77 (1): 251–86.

Pennycock, Alistair. 2013. *Cultural Politics of English as an International Language*. New York: Routledge.

Pérez Huber, Lindsay. 2010. "Using Latina/o Critical Race Theory (LatLit) and Racist Nativism to Explore Intersectionality in the Educational Experiences of Undocumented Chicana College Students." *Educational Foundations* 24 (1/2): 77–96.

Petrescu, Camelia. 2015. "Translating Ideology: A Teaching Challenge." *Procedia: Social and Behavioral Sciences* 191 (June): 2721–25.

Power, Robert C. 2012. *Strategies and Techniques for Teaching Constitutional Law*. New York: Wolters Kluwer Law and Business.

Radzilowski, John. 2009. "Immigration and Ethnicity across the History Curriculum." *Journal of American Ethnic History* 28 (2): 82–86.

Ranciere, Jacques. 1991. *The Ignorant Schoolmaster: Five Lessons in Intellectual Emancipation*. Stanford: Stanford University Press.

Rao, Nagesh. 1995. "The Oh No! Syndrome: A Language Expectation Model of Undergraduate Negative Reactions toward Foreign Teaching Assistants." Paper presented at the 79th annual meeting of the International Communication Association, Albuquerque, New Mexico, May 25–29.

Rapold, Nicolas. 2013. "500 Days in a Cave: The Safest Refuge." *New York Times*, April 4. Accessed on June 27, 2016. http://www.nytimes.com/2013/04/05/movies/no-place-on-earth-a-documentary-by-janet-tobias.html?_r=0.

Rasmussen, Amy Cabrera. 2014. "Toward an Intersectional Political Science Pedagogy." *Journal of Political Science Education* 10 (1): 102–16.

Remer, Pam, and Rory Remer. 2000. "The Alien Invasion Exercise: Creating an Experience of Diversity." *International Journal of Action Methods: Psychodrama, Skill Training, and Role Playing* 52 (4): 147–54.

Richards, Jack C., John Platt, and Heidi Platt. 1992. *Longman Dictionary of Language Teaching and Applied Linguistics*. 2nd ed. Harlem, UK: Longman.

Roark, James L., Michael P. Johnson, Patricia C. Cohen, Sarah Stage, Alan Lawson, and Susan Hartmann. 2011. *Understanding the American Promise*. Vol. 2. New York: Bedford St. Martin's.

Rose, Charlie. 2008. *Georgia and Russia*. Charlie Rose, LLC, DVD.

Rosette, Ashleigh S., Geoffrey J. Leonardelli, and Katherine W. Phillips. 2008. "The White Standard: Racial Bias in Leader Categorization." *Journal of Applied Psychology* 93 (4): 758–77.

Ross, Jannell. 2015. "Obama Says Liberal College Students Should Not Be 'Coddled': Are We Really Surprised?" *Washington Post*, September 15. Accessed June 25, 2016. https://www.washingtonpost.com/news/the-fix/wp/2015/09/15/obama-says-liberal-college-students-should-not-be-coddled-are-we-really-surprised/?tid=a_inl.

Rothberg, Michael. 2001. "W. E. B. DuBois in Warsaw: Holocaust Memory and the Color Line, 1949–1952." *Yale Journal of Criticism* 14 (1): 169–89.

Russell, Susan H., Mary P. Hancock, and James McCullough. 2007. "Benefits of Undergraduate Research Experiences." *Science* 316 (5824): 548–49.

Sanders, Chris. 2006. "Censorship 101: Anti-Hazelwood Laws and the Preservation of Free Speech at Colleges and Universities." *Alabama Law Review* 58 (1): 159–78.

Sarin, Vic, dir. 2007. *Partition*. Woodland Hills, CA: Allumination, DVD.

Schechter, Hava, and Gavriel Salomon. 2005. "Does Vicarious Experience of Suffering Affect Empathy for an Adversary? The Effects of Israeli's Visits to Auschwitz on Their Empathy for Palestinians." *Journal of Peace Education* 2 (2): 125–38.

Schmidt, Patrick. 2004. "An Approach to Diversity Training in Canada." *Industrial and Commercial Training* 36 (4): 148–52.

Schulz, Renate A. 2007. "The Challenge of Assessing Cultural Understanding in the Context of Foreign Language Instruction." *Foreign Language Annals* 40 (1): 9–26.

Scottish Documentary Institute. 2007. "The Unbearable Whiteness of Being." Accessed June 28, 2016. http://www.scottishdocinstitute.com/films/the-unbearable-whiteness-of-being.

Sharplin, Elaine. 2009. "Bringing Them In: The Experiences of Imported and Overseas-Qualified Teachers." *Australian Journal of Education* 53 (2): 192–206.

Shaw, Carolyn M. 2010. "Designing and Using Simulations and Role-Playing Exercises." In *The International Studies Encyclopedia*, edited by Robert A. Denemark. Hoboken, NJ: Wiley-Blackwell. Accessed June 25, 2016. http://webs.wichita.edu/depttools/depttoolsmemberfiles/carolynshaw/Shaw%20in%20Compendium.pdf.

Sherriff, Lucy. 2015. "Staffordshire University Apologises for Accusing Student on Counter-Terrorism Course of Terrorism." *Huffington Post*, September 24. Accessed June 29, 2016. http://www.huffingtonpost.co.uk/2015/09/24/staffordshire-university-accuses-student-terrorism-reading-book_n_8188228.html.

Shrewsbury, Carolyn M. 1993. "What Is Feminist Pedagogy?" *Women's Studies Quarterly* 21 (3/4): 8–16.

Simpson, Robin, and Karen Ballard. 2005. "What Is Being Assessed in the MRCGP Oral Examination?" *British Journal of General Practice* 55 (515): 430–36.

Sinclair, Upton. 1906. *The Jungle*. New York: Grosset and Dunlap.

Sion, Brigitte. 2014. *Death Tourism: Disaster Sites as Recreational Landscapes*. London: Seagull Books.

Smith, Bettye P., and Juanita Johnson-Bailey. 2011. "Student Ratings of Teaching Effectiveness: Implications for Non-White Women in the Academy." *Negro Educational Review* 62 (1–4): 115–40.

Smith, Janice A., Colleen M. Meyers, and Amy J. Burkhalter. 1992. *Communicate: Strategies for International Teaching Assistants*. Englewood Cliffs, NJ: Regents/Prentice Hall.

Smith, Pete, and Chris Rust. 2011. "The Potential for Research Based Learning for the Creation of Truly Inclusive Academic Communities of Practice." *Innovations in Education and Teaching International* 48 (2): 115–25.

Smith, Stephen. 2007. "Teaching about the Holocaust in the Setting of Museums and Memorials." In *Testimony, Tensions, and Tikkun: Teaching the Holocaust in Colleges and Universities*, edited by Myrna Goldenberg and Rochelle L. Millen, 271–83. Seattle: University of Washington Press.

Sobel, David. 1998. *Mapmaking with Children: Sense of Place Education for the Elementary Years*. Portsmouth, NH: Heinemann.

Sterling, Stephen. 2007. "Riding the Storm: Towards a Connective Cultural Consciousness." In *Social Learning towards a Sustainable World: Principles, Perspectives, and Praxis*, edited by Arjen E. J. Wals, 63–82. Wageningen, the Netherlands: Wageningen Academic Publishers.

Stevenson, Robert Louis. 1993. *Treasure Island*. Mineola, NY: Dover.

StoryCorps. n.d. Accessed June 27, 2016. https://storycorps.org.

Suárez-Orozco, Carola, Saskias Casanova, Margary Martin, Dalal Katsiaficas, Veronica Cuellar, Naila Antonia Smith, and Sandra Isabel Dias. 2015. "Toxic Rain in Class: Classroom Interpersonal Microaggressions." *Educational Researcher* 44 (3): 151–60.

Sue, Derald Wing. 2015. *Race Talk and the Conspiracy of Silence*. Hoboken, NJ: John Wiley and Sons.

Sue, Derald W., Christina M. Capodilupo, Gina C. Torino, Jennifer M. Bucerri, Aisha M. B. Holder, Kevin L. Nadal, and Marta E. Esquilin. 2007. "Racial Microaggressions in Everyday Life: Implications for Clinical Practice." *American Psychologist* 62 (4): 271–86.

Sue, Derald Wing, Annie I. Lin, Gina C. Torino, Christina C. Capodilupo, and David P. Rivera. 2009. "Racial Micro-Aggressions and Difficult Dialogues in the Classroom." *Cultural Diversity and Ethnic Minority Psychology* 15 (2): 183–90.

Tedrow, Barbara, and Reitumetse Mabokela. 2006. "Implementing Teaching Reforms at a New University in South Africa." *International Journal of Education Reform* 15 (1): 56–79.

Thomas, Gloria D., and Carol Hollenshead. 2001. "Resisting from the Margins: The Coping Strategies of Black Women and Other Women of Color Faculty Members at a Research University." *Journal of Negro Education* 70 (3): 166–75.

Thomas, Kecia M., Ny M. Tran, and Bryan L. Dawson. 2011. "An Inclusive Strategy of Teaching Diversity." *Advances in Developing Human Resources* 12 (3): 295–311.

Thomas A. Edison, Inc. 1903. "Ghetto Fish Market." *Library of Congress Digital Collection.* Accessed June 27, 2016. http://www.loc.gov/item/00694374.

Tolkien, John Ronald Reuel. 1966. *The Hobbit.* New York: Ballantine Books.

Totten, Samuel, and Eric Markusen. 2006. *Genocide in Darfur: Investigating the Atrocities in the Sudan.* New York: Routledge.

Trigg, Dylan. 2009. "The Place of Trauma: Memory, Hauntings, and the Temporality of Ruins." *Memory Studies* 2 (1): 87–101.

Tsesis, Alexander. 2010. "Burning Crosses on Campus: University Hate Speech Codes." *Connecticut Law Review* 43 (December): 617–72.

Turner, Caroline Sotello Vierner. 2002. "Women of Color in Academe: Living with Multiple Marginality." *Journal of Higher Education* 73 (1): 74–93.

U.S. Census Bureau. n.d. "Gwinnett County, Georgia." *State and County Quickfacts.* Accessed June 25, 2016. http://quickfacts.census.gov/qfd/states/13/13135.html.

U.S. Courts. n.d. "Background—*Mendez v. Westminster* Re-enactment." Accessed June 26, 2016. http://www.uscourts.gov/educational-resources/educational-activities/background-mendez-v-westminster-re-enactment.

Valentine, Gill. 2007. "Theorizing and Researching Intersectionality: A Challenge for Feminist Geography." *Professional Geographer* 59 (1): 10–21.

van Dijk, Teun A. 2013. "Ideology and Discourse." In *The Oxford Handbook of Political Ideologies*, edited by Michael Freeden and Lyman Tower Sargent, 175–96. Oxford: Oxford University Press.

Vargas, Lucila, ed. 2002. *Women Faculty of Color in the White Classroom: Narratives on the Pedagogical Implications of Teacher Diversity.* New York: Peter Lang.

Vecchio, Diane C. 2004. "Immigrant and Ethnic History in the United States Survey." *History Teacher* 37 (4): 494–500.

Waldron, Jeremy. 2010. "Dignity and Defamation: The Visibility of Hate." *Harvard Law Review* 123 (7): 1596–1657.

Wallace, Chloe. 2010. "Using Oral Assessment to Improve Student Learning in Law." *Law Teacher* 44 (3): 367–77.

Weber, Lynn. 1998. "A Conceptual Framework for Understanding Race, Class, Gender, and Sexuality." *Psychology of Women Quarterly* 22 (1): 13–22.

Wollaston, Isabel. 2005. "Negotiating the Marketplace: The Role(s) of Holocaust Museums Today." *Journal of Modern Jewish Studies* 4 (1): 63–80.

Wong, David. 2012. "Curiosity Is Not Good—But It's Not Bad, Either." *Phi Delta Kappan* 93 (8): 61–65.

World Bank. 2015. *Migration and Development Brief 24.* Accessed June 29, 2016. http://econ.worldbank.org/WBSITE/EXTERNAL/EXTDEC/EXTDECPROSPECTS/0,,contentMDK:21125572~pagePK:64165401~piPK:64165026~theSitePK:476883,00.html.

Wysok, Wiesław. 2013. "The Principles of Cooperation between Museum Pedagogical Staff at Memorial Sites and Teachers in Carrying Out Educational Projects: Practical Remarks." In *Educational Visits to the State Museum at Majdanek: A Guide for Teachers*, edited by Tomasz Kranz, 65–75. Lublin: Państwowe Muzeum na Majdanku.

Yang, June, and Douglas Laube. 1983. "Improvement of Reliability of an Oral Assessment by a Structured Evaluation Instrument." *Academic Medicine* 58 (11): 864–72.

Yannakogeorgos, Panayotis A. 2014. "Rethinking the Threat of Cyberterrorism." In *Cyberterrorism: Understanding, Assessment, and Response*, edited by Tom M. Chen, Lee Jarvis, and Stuart Macdonald, 43–62. Berlin: Springer.

Yezierska, Anzia. 1975. *Bread Givers*. 3rd ed. New York: Persea Books.

———. 1987. *Red Ribbon on a White Horse*. New York: Persea Books.

———. 2012. *Hungry Hearts*. Charleston, SC: Forgotten Books.

Zakaria, Fareed. 2007. *The Future of Freedom: Illiberal Democracy at Home and Abroad*. New York: W. W. Norton.

Zembylas, Michalinos. 2008. "Trauma, Justice and the Politics of Emotion: The Violence of Sentimentality in Education." *Discourse: Studies in the Cultural Politics of Education* 29 (1): 1–17.

Zinsser, William Knowlton. 2006. *Writing to Learn*. New York: Harper and Row.

Index

About the Authors

Natalie Bormann, PhD, is in the Political Science Department at Northeastern University, where she teaches courses on genocides and political thought. She leads a study abroad program on Holocaust studies that takes students to Germany and Poland each summer. Her research explores the interplay of trauma, memory, and ethics, which she addresses in her forthcoming monograph on *The Ethics of Teaching at Sties of Trauma and Violence: Student Encounters with the Holocaust*.

Scott A. Boykin, MTS, JD, PhD, is an associate professor of political science at Georgia Gwinnett College. Before joining Georgia Gwinnett College, Dr. Boykin practiced law in Alabama and Texas and served as a judicial clerk to Judge Patrick E. Higginbotham on the U.S. Court of Appeals for the Fifth Circuit. Boykin has published research in political theory and American constitutional law.

Dovilė Budrytė, PhD, is a professor of political science at Georgia Gwinnett College. Her publications include articles about the Baltic states and three books, *Taming Nationalism? Political Community Building in the Post–Soviet Baltic States* (2005), *Feminist Conversations: Women, Trauma and Empowerment in Post–Transitional Societies* (coedited with Lisa M. Vaughn and Natalya T. Riegg, 2009), and *Memory and Trauma in International Relations: Theories, Cases and Debates* (coedited with Erica Resende, 2013). In 2014–2015, she was the recipient of the University System of Georgia Excellence in Teaching Award. Her research interests include intersectionality, memory politics, and trauma education.

Veronica Czastkiewicz teaches political science at Pueblo Community College. She has also held teaching positions at Northeastern University and Cornell College. Her research focuses on political rhetoric, problem definition, and public policy framing.

Bryan L. Dawson, PhD, is an assistant professor in the Department of Psychological Science at the University of North Georgia. He teaches introductory psychology, psychological science, quantitative methods, and various leadership seminars. Dawson's research focuses on discrimination and the attitudinal and behavioral effects of positive and negative beliefs toward women, people of color, and LGBTQ people. He is working on projects investigating perceptions of gender, gender and ethnic discrimination, and perceptions of video games.

Josephine J. Dawuni, PhD, is an assistant professor of political science at Howard University, Washington, DC. Her primary areas of research include judicial politics, gender and the law, international human rights, women's civil society organizing, and democratization. She is the editor (with Gretchen Bauer) of *Gender and the Judiciary in Africa: From Obscurity to Parity?* (2016). She is working on a second book (coedited with Akua Kuenyehia and Leigh Swigart), *African Women Judges on International Courts: Untold Stories* (2017). Her works have appeared in such journals as *Studies in Gender and Development in Africa, Journal of African Law*, and *Africa Today*. Her areas of teaching are largely anchored between comparative politics and international relations, with a focus on gender and the law, African politics, and international human rights.

Ignas Kalpokas, PhD, is a lecturer at Vytautas Magnus University (Lithuania). Kalpokas's main research and teaching areas include international relations and international political theory, primarily with respect to sovereignty and globalization of norms; identity and formation of political communities; and political use of social media and cyber security in general. He is also interested in public international law and legal theory.

Michael A. Lewkowicz, PhD, is an assistant professor of political science at Georgia Gwinnett College. His academic interests cover a variety of topics in American politics, including political behavior, election laws, political participation, governmental institutions, constitutional law, and public policy.

Kristina Watkins Mormino, PhD, is an associate professor of French, coordinator of the Global Studies Certification Program, and senior mentor for the School of Liberal Arts at Georgia Gwinnett College. Her research has focused on medieval French texts—by and about women—especially those featuring virgin martyrs, and the teaching of culture in foreign language courses.

Ellen G. Rafshoon, PhD, is an associate professor of history and an assistant dean at Georgia Gwinnett College. She teaches recent American history. Her research examines the role of Atlanta's activists and medical professionals in the reproductive rights movement.

Janita L. Rawls, PhD, is an associate professor of management at Georgia Gwinnett College, and her research focus is in the areas of assessment and teaching pedagogy. Her publications consist of several coauthored articles, including "Does Delivery Format Make a Difference in Learning about Global and Cultural Understanding?" and "Are You Talking to Me? On the Use of Oral Examinations in Undergraduate Business Courses." In 2016, she won the Georgia Gwinnett College School of Business, Scholarship in Teaching and Learning Award. She is a board of trustees member for the Academy of Business Education.

Richard S. Rawls, PhD, is a professor of history at Georgia Gwinnett College. He researches ancient and medieval topics. Recent publications include "The Visigothic Kingdom" in *The Encyclopedia of Empire* (2015) and "The Rain Miracle of Marcus Aurelius and the Early Christian Community" in *A Dangerous Mind* (edited by W. Johnston and D. Crosby, 2015). He is writing a paper on oral examinations in undergraduate history classes, and he serves as a deep facilitator, training faculty in internationalizing courses at Georgia Gwinnett College.

Natalya T. Riegg, PhD, is chair of the History, Political Science, and Global Studies department at the University of Saint Mary in Kansas. Riegg has authored two books and dozens of articles. She is a member of the Russian International Academy of Humanitarian Sciences and a former fellow at the Maison des Sciences de l'Homme in Paris and was a professor and NGO leader in her native Armenia. Since 1992, when she worked with Armenian and Azerbaijani women to build a cross-national dialogue of peace and reconciliation during their countries' war over Nagorno-Karabakh, Riegg has been a constant contributor of practical and theory-based approaches to conflict resolution.

Louis Schmier, PhD, is a professor of history, emeritus, at Valdosta State University in South Georgia, where he taught for forty-six years until his retirement in December 2012. A noted authority on the Southern Jewish experience, he is a founder of the Southern Jewish Historical Society, recipient of numerous grants, and author of several books and innumerable articles.

He is also a renowned teacher, with more than one thousand reflective essays on the subject, some of which have been published in four anthologies. Between 2006 and 2012, he taught classes dealing with the Holocaust at Valdosta State University, as well as at Zhengzhou University in Zhengzhou, China, and Henan University in Kaifang, China, during his university's Study Abroad Program. He was a consultant on the Holocaust in Henan University's Jewish Studies Program. Since retirement, aside from spoiling his grandchildren, he has been working on several books, among which is one detailing the unique way in which he taught Holocaust classes.

Barbara Tedrow, PhD, is from western Pennsylvania. Her family, originally from Eastern Europe, has lived in the United States for three generations. As a first-generation college student, Barbara earned her graduate degrees with a concentration in social studies and diversity issues. Her public school professional experiences included teaching, administration, and higher education research in Michigan, Georgia (United States), Kenya, and South Africa. In 2002–2003, she was awarded a teaching and research grant to South Africa as a Core Fulbright Scholar. In 2008, she returned to South Africa as a Fulbright specialist at Rhodes and Fort Hare Universities, where she consulted with lecturers to examine ways to decolonize the curriculum. For fall 2016 and fall 2017, Barbara Tedrow was awarded a Fulbright Specialist Grant to consult with university faculty in Lithuania as they confront postcolonial issues after decades of Soviet rule.

www.ingramcontent.com/pod-product-compliance
Lightning Source LLC
Chambersburg PA
CBHW030338030726
47499CB00003B/829